Odyssey on the Sea of Faith

Don Cupitt at Aston Clinton, Buckinghamshire, England
29 December 1963 — his wedding day

Odyssey on the Sea of Faith

The Life & Writings of Don Cupitt

Nigel Leaves

Odyssey on the Sea of Faith: The Life & Writings of Don Cupitt

Published in 2004 by Polebridge Press, P.O. Box 6144, Santa Rosa, California 95406.

Copyright © 2004 by Nigel Leaves

ISBN 0-944344-62-3

Library of Congress Cataloging-in-Publication Data

Leaves, Nigel, 1958-
    Odyssey on the sea of faith : the life & writings of Don Cupitt / by Nigel Leaves.
      p. cm.
    Based on the author's thesis (Ph. D.)--Murdoch University, 2001.
    Includes bibliographical references (p.) and index.
    ISBN 0-944344-62-3
    1. Cupitt, Don 2. Church of England--Clergy--Biography. 3. Anglican
    Communion--England--Clergy--Biography. I. Title.

BX5199.C87L43 2003
230'.3'092--dc22

                                                                      2003066354

Contents

Foreword

Most of what has been written about me so far has been written by fellow Anglican priests — many of them friends — impelled to write by a consciousness of having much in common with me and by an anxiety to have it known by all that they do nevertheless very definitely differ from me. The first books, by Keith Ward (*Holding Fast to God*) and Brian Hebblethwaite (*The Ocean of Truth*), were written as straight refutations. The first critical study was a short dissertation by Scott Cowdell (*Atheist Priest? Don Cupitt and Christianity*). Cowdell's work established the pattern of trying to explain me by setting out to reconstruct the development of my thinking from the published evidence — something I have tried (with rather mixed results) to do myself. I have been boiling with ideas for thirty years, and have usually been too close to my own work and in too much of a hurry to be able to see clearly which ideas are dogs, which are turkeys, and which are good and worth pursuing. Cowdell, writing from Brisbane and without contacting me, could take a more detached view. Stephen Ross White (*Don Cupitt and the Future of Christian Doctrine*) was still more detached: I have not met him even yet.

Now Nigel Leaves has gone one better. In the year 2000 he presented an enormous Ph.D. dissertation about me to Murdoch University at Perth, Western Australia. One Australian examiner, after reluctantly acknowledging the thoroughness of Leaves's study of my thirty-odd books, together with all the articles and reviews and the radio and television work, was reduced to complaining that Leaves's treatment of my journalism for the London *Guardian* was skimpy, which struck me as academic gamesmanship of a very high order. How do all these Australians know more about me than I know about myself? Perhaps we should invert the Gospel saying and declare that a prophet is most honoured by those who live furthest away from him.

Meanwhile in Britain a book or article saying what's wrong with Cupitt and why you need not trouble actually to read him has become recognized as a very sound career move. Keith Ward's 1982 book coincided with his appointment to a Chair in London, and was speedily followed by his elevation to the Regius Professorship at Oxford. Rowan Williams published an essay 'On Not Quite Agreeing with Don Cupitt' in the first number of *Modern Theology* (1984) and then began his ascent, to a Chair at Oxford in 1986, to a bishopric in 1992, and to the first of his archbishoprics soon after. Indeed, the upper echelons of both the Church and the Academy are packed with people who used to know me, but now know me no more. Yet the differences between me and my eminent former friends are often not great: please don't tell his Evangelical tormentors, but there are passages in Rowan Williams that sound surprisingly like me. I find that rather shocking, don't you?

With Nigel Leaves I come oddly full circle. My first New Testament and Greek teacher was C.A. Pierce, then Chaplain of Magdalene College, Cambridge. In 1956 Tony Pierce moved to Perth with the task of establishing the first Anglican theological college in Western Australia, to be called Wollaston College. He wrote in 1959 asking me to join him. I was 25 and scarcely yet even ordained, but I had already been made to promise to return to Westcott House, Cambridge, where I was lined up to follow Bob Runcie and John Habgood as Vice-Principal. At 25 I was not merely respectable, but even sought-after. I had as many offers as a pretty girl. So I had to decline my first invitation to Australia; but today Nigel Leaves is the Director at Wollaston College, and I have lately stayed there and lectured at his invitation — making belated amends after some 44 years. Sadly, his recent death robbed me of the chance to track down and salute Tony Pierce himself.

You will have gathered that I am what in England is called a wrong 'un — a suspect horse. But I am not for a moment complaining. In my recent writing I have even gone to the opposite extreme and have tried to eliminate 'The Problem of Evil' from my world-view, completely revaluing the traditional 'metaphysical evil' (temporality, contingency and finitude), and teaching that we must learn to say a wholehearted Amen to our own lives. Like the animals that we are, we should love life and not moan. So I personally am not complaining about anything, even though it is true (as the published record sufficiently shows) that my intellectual and personal history has been quite exceptionally, and almost uniquely, turbulent. However, living continuously in a state of high intellectual excitement and often acute crisis has its own very special consolations. Indeed, the happiness has sometimes been far greater than could ever be found in any amount of social and religious respectability. For that reason I have sometimes said that I have wanted to teach people that religious thought is possible, and is intensely rewarding.

It is still true, though, that in Britain I have been in deep trouble for twenty-five years, and the chief problem has been my incorrigible rationalism. (After all, nobody in British religion ever got into trouble for being irrational, which is normal, and is expected.) In Britain there are two views about religious truth: one is that we don't need ever to question it, because it is known already, and in full (to my denomination, you will understand). The other view is that all religion is simply irrational, and there is no need ever to give the subject any serious thought. These two views are politically entirely acceptable, because neither of them threatens to change anything. Everyone can remain in their present position, and nobody needs to do any thinking at all.

My own view, however, is awkward for everybody. It is that the modern critical study of religion has put it beyond doubt that religion everywhere is just a human creation, and as such remains very important to us, even after philosophical and historical criticism have demolished all our received religious beliefs. To get ourselves into a better position, we need a lot of hard thinking and readiness to accept both personal and institutional change. This will not be easy, but the rewards will be proportionately great; and surely every human being before he or she dies would wish to make some personal effort to reach a considered view on the great questions of life? What are we, what is our world, what can we know, how should we live, what is the best we can hope for? — It's not crazy to be preoccupied with questions like these, and to pursue them determinedly . . . is it? Unfortunately, in Britain too much honesty in pursuing such questions can be seen as deeply threatening by many people and by many established interests that are still committed to traditional answers to them.

Nigel Leaves in this first volume has made the best attempt so far to trace the development of the main themes of my thinking to date. He has aimed (as I have always aimed) to write in a way intelligible to the general reader. Even I can understand him, and he has made me wonder about my own view of what I have been up to. I tend not to describe myself as a theologian, because for most people 'theology' means simply ecclesiastical theology — which in my view is now a dead subject. So I usually call myself a philosopher, or 'a religious thinker who has specialized on the creative side'. Sometimes I say that I'm 'an experimental religious writer'. Nigel Leaves, however, in his big dissertation particularly foregrounded my ethics and religion, and he will I understand be dealing with these topics in his second volume. And he does think of what I have done as being theology — perhaps because like George Pattison he sees me as having tried to widen the range of what can count as being theology.

So I thank Nigel Leaves for the shrewdness with which he has picked out the chief threads running through my writing. I thank him too for his thoroughness, because not everyone takes such care. Recently I had to attend a conference about Don Cupitt, and found that it was exactly like being able to hear from inside the coffin the proceedings at one's own funeral. There I was, listening to myself being talked about, hearing much I disagreed with, and being unable to butt in because it had been decreed that I was to be silent for the day. On this present occasion I have actually been invited to put my oar in; but there is much less need to do so. Thanks then to Nigel Leaves for what he has done here, and more power to his elbow as he takes up his pen for a second volume.

Don Cupitt
Emmanuel College
CAMBRIDGE

Preface

Odyssey on the Sea of Faith and my forthcoming book (*Surfing on the Sea of Faith*) had their genesis as a Ph.D. thesis presented to Murdoch University, Western Australia in 2001. Thus Don Cupitt has occupied my waking (and I expect sleeping) moments for the last six or so years. It has been a pleasurable experience, though not without its challenges, least of all because of Don Cupitt's phenomenal capacity to produce a new book every six months. I have adopted the role of an ancient seer trying to foresee the next move by this original and brilliant thinker. Like the fortune-teller that I encountered as a child when the traveling-fair arrived at my hometown sometimes I forecast correctly and frequently I was way off beam! Who could have predicted the sudden turn to Heidegger or analysis of the theology of everyday speech? But then, Don Cupitt is no ordinary writer content to sit back and accept the accolades for having produced *the* definitive theological classic. He is a spiritual wanderer, restlessly creating new religious thought in our postmodern world where nothing is static and where we can free ourselves from the constraints of orthodoxy.

Obviously for such a lengthy project over a number of years has meant that I have been indebted to many people. Firstly, I owe much gratitude to Don Cupitt for not only providing inspiration for this assignment but also his support and encouragement in so many ways, too numerous to mention here. He has proved to be an excellent subject for a researcher. Secondly, none of this would have happened without the initial financial assistance of the Anglican Diocese of Perth and their granting me the Sambell Memorial scholarship. In particular, I thank the Primate of the Anglican Church of Australia, the Most Reverend Dr P.F. Carnley AO. Thirdly, I was fortunate to learn much about how Cupitt's writings have influenced many people throughout the world by those within the Sea of Faith Networks. I mention David Simmers, the Reverend Ronald Pearse, Gregory Spearitt, Judith and Peter Bore, Janet Trisk and Hugo Vitalis, together with countless others who have contributed to the widening of my perceptions of the Sea of Faith.

It was on the recommendation of two of my Ph.D. examiners — Lloyd Geering and Ronald Nicolson — that I pursued the idea of turning a thesis into books accessible to the general public. I thank Robert Funk of Polebridge Press for seeing the value in such an exercise and his care and solicitude for a young author.

To my wife and young son Sebastian go my deepest thanks. Julie has helped me more than perhaps she realizes — by not only remaining in full-time employment when I returned to life as a student, but also by her wholehearted (albeit sometimes bemused) support during all the highs and lows of research. Likewise, Sebastian grew accustomed to his dad being locked in his study unable to play the games with dinosaurs and lego that so preoccupy a young boy. To Julie and Sebastian this volume is dedicated, with much gratitude and love.

Introduction

Don Cupitt belongs in the theological hall of fame. He is an original, radical, and controversial contemporary Christian author. Cupitt regards his writings as a flowing project that is always changing. More than thirty years ago he set out on a journey without any predetermined destination. Since then his task has been to discover the degree to which it is possible to express *new* religious thought and belief in the late twentieth and early twenty-first centuries.

Cupitt's writings have passed through seven stages, beginning from just before the publication of his most controversial and (in)famous book, *Taking Leave of God*, in 1980. While that book has now been elevated to the status of "classic" by its publisher, Cupitt has today moved a long way from the theological and ecclesiastical viewpoints expressed therein. It is perhaps his most recent writings, which have received only cursory attention in print, that best outline a faith that many, especially those on the edges of Christianity, might embrace with integrity and a sense of liberation. The seven stages can be set out in diagram form (figure 1) showing the linear progression of his thought. The stages expose a "string of selves" that has now arrived at a personal religious outlook with which is he fairly content. Cupitt's theology has undergone almost seismic changes over the course of his literary career, most of which has been conducted within the public domain. Hence one must always be very specific concerning which phase of Cupitt's theology one is speaking of, and which of his seven stages of writing one is debating!

It can be seen in figure 1 that Cupitt's writings have gone from "negative theology" (stage 1) to "the religion of the future" (stage 7). Each of these stages reflects the questions of many people who seek a religious faith that is both credible and able to respond satisfactorily to the difficulties raised by postmodernism, social and literary theory, and the demise of traditional Christianity. What does the word "God" mean? Can Christianity be rescued from the iron grip of Platonism that has kept it so authoritarian and dogmatic that converts must assent to an Orthodoxy that in many cases appears unworkable or anti-life? What will the religion of the future be? Where can we find a religious outlook that is new, honest and satisfying? Can Christianity be reformed before it dies a natural death? Or, if we leave the dead to bury their dead, what shall we put in its place?

Cupitt's seven-stage odyssey is like a roller-coaster ride. It consists of many furious twists and turns, all conducted at high speed and with dizzying effects. It goes from liberal Christian through radical Christian-

---
Figure one

THE SEVEN STAGES OF DON CUPITT'S WRITINGS
"Of which Cupitt are you speaking?"[1]

Stage 1: (1971–1979) The Negative Theology   (9 books)

    Christ and the Hiddenness of God (1971)
    Crisis of Moral Authority (1972)
    The Leap of Reason (1976)
    The Worlds of Science and Religion (1976)
    Who was Jesus? (1977)
    Explorations in Theology (1979)
    The Nature of Man (1979)
    The Debate about Christ (1979)
    Jesus and the Gospel of God (1979)

Stage 2: (1980–1985) Non-realism – "Coming Out"   (4 books)

    Taking Leave of God (1980)
    The World to Come (1982)
    The Sea of Faith (1984)
    Only Human (1985)

Stage 3: (1986–1989) Postmodernism and Anti-realism   (4 books)

    Life Lines (1986)
    The Long-Legged Fly (1987)
    The New Christian Ethics (1988)
    Radicals and the Future of the Church (1989)

Stage 4: (1990–1997) Expressionism (8 books)

Creation out of Nothing (1990) (1 booklet)
What Is a Story? (1991)
The Time Being (1992)
Rethinking Religion (1992) (booklet)
After All (1994)
The Last Philosophy (1995)
Solar Ethics (1995)
After God (1997)
Mysticism after Modernity (1997)

Stage 5: (1998) The Turn to Be-ing (2 books)

The Religion of Being (1998)
The Revelation of Being (1998)

Stage 6: (1999–2000) Ordinary Language (3 books)

The New Religion of Life in Everyday Speech (1999)
The Meaning of It All in Everyday Speech (1999)
Kingdom Come in Everyday Speech (2000)

Stage 7: (2000 onwards) The Religion of the Future (4 books)

Philosophy's Own Religion (2000) (1 selected essays)
Reforming Christianity (2001)
Emptiness and Brightness (2001)
Is Nothing Sacred? (2002) (selected essays)
Life, Life (2003)

Buddhist to a position he now describes as "empty radical humanist." Cupitt is not a systematic writer but follows the advice of the postmodern writers "to go with the flow" and venture upon new avenues of religious thought. Faith and religious exploration admit of no boundaries. He casts himself into a boat, throws out the life jackets, slips his mooring lines, and explores unchartered waters on the sea of faith, inviting others to do the same!

In the first stage Cupitt was firmly rooted in liberal Christianity, and his main concern was to question and search after the Truth. He used 'capital-T' Truth for the kind of objective truth that religion and dogmatic metaphysics had in the past championed. Very much as the popular American theologian Bishop John Shelby Spong does today, he argued that beyond all the flawed human images of deity there was an objective reality (God) that was greater and more mysterious than could be captured in words or images. Indeed, it was only by deconstructing or abandoning these imperfect descriptions that one would be able to affirm with Spong (echoing Paul Tillich) "the God beyond theism." This is not a new idea in theology; it was expressed by many negative or apophatic theologians, especially such Christian mystical writers as St. John of the Cross (1542–1591), who have argued that we cannot say what God is, but only what God is not. Accordingly, Cupitt followed the negative way by admitting that the Divine was ultimately ineffable, or a mystery. God is neither this nor that, but lies beyond language. But all was not lost, for people still had access to God through the work and person of Jesus as recorded in the Gospels. It was Jesus who had revealed the nature of the Divine Being and through whom one could glimpse something of the "hiddenness" of God.

However, unlike Spong and some of the mystics, the apophatic way eventually led Cupitt beyond mystery and silence to Nothing (No Thing). All language about God was anthropocentric (human-centred) and if we use human language to describe God then God is, in effect, a human creation. Therefore, instead of affirming Someone/Something outside this world, Cupitt set out on a long journey of exploration which led to him to embrace the Death of God, the outsidelessness of our existence, the end of metaphysics and foundationalism, and the advent of nihilism. He was confronted with the predicament that the German philosopher Georg Hegel had described in the nineteenth century, namely that the world had begun to recognize the God in whom it had put its faith as a deity of its own creation. Indeed, some like Friedrich Nietzsche took it a step further: outside the sphere of human biological existence, he said, exist no God, no heaven or hell, no mind and no language. Nor do we live in a cosmos, a world ready-made to be explored and understood by us. In short, our world is of our own making: it is "empty" or "outsideless," and we must live without the support of dogmatic realism (especially about God), for *we* are and have to be the Creators.

While this nihilism, radical humanism or universal emptiness might terrify some people (as indeed it did Nietzsche, and may have been responsible for his descent into insanity in 1889), Cupitt took the opposite view: we must love and find religious meaning in a world without God. We must pass through the fire and terror of nihilism — the recognition that "all this is all there is" — to new religious thought and expression that can cope with transitoriness and relativism.

These thoughts propelled him into his second and best-known stage. This is exemplified by his book *Taking Leave of God*, and it culminated in his promulgation of a non-realist doctrine of God. Cupitt was indebted to the philosopher Immanuel Kant, who had argued that we need to construct a theory of knowledge without having any recourse to a Divine Being as guarantor of objectivity. Human beings could, he insisted, make perfectly good sense of their world without any help from "above." Thus Cupitt put forward the notion that people must give up the realist idea of an all-powerful God "out-there" who sustains and creates the Universe. The word "God" need not be abandoned, however, for it was still a helpful fiction that could be put to profitable use. He proposed that when people used the word "God" they referred to a spiritual ideal; the word did not name a metaphysical Being, but the concept could help people live *religiously*. Such a way of living would blend the ethics of Christianity with the spirituality of Buddhism and could be described as a kind of "godless morality." Cupitt was at this time close to existentialist theologians like Rudolf Bultmann and Paul Tillich. Christian doctrines were not to be understood literally, but interpreted in terms of the way of life that they recommended. To believe in God as Creator, for example, was to understand one's existence as pure and gracious gift; and to live a risen life was to proclaim: "Christ is risen — in me!" Cupitt was not so much changing Christian doctrines as translating them into rules of life, in the way that the philosopher Ludwig Wittgenstein had advised. The non-realist interpretation of Christian doctrine that Cupitt was advocating in the 1980s is set forth in figure 2. Still, Cupitt was not content simply to revise Christian doctrines and theology; he also advocated philosophical non-realism or anti-realism, and this agenda became Stage 3 of his writing.

Philosophical non-realism or anti-realism was inspired by a re-reading of the works of Nietzsche and the implementation of postmodern ideas. If there is no objective God, there is also no objective Truth. There are only 'truths,' or as Nietzsche famously expressed it, "There are no facts, only interpretations." It is in and through language that people construct their reality. There is no vision of *the* world, only *our* world and how we understand that world in the light of our current ideas and theories. Language is also transactional, with all meanings and values shifting and changing as people's language changes. By changing the way that people speak and think (thoughts are merely unspoken words), i.e. by altering language, the world changes too. People become creators and co-creators of their own world(s).

Pursuing this anti-realist emphasis on interpretation or "spin" to its logical conclusion led Cupitt into his fourth stage — Expressionism. If there is no absolute Origin, no last end, and no objective reality, value, or

─────────── **Figure two** ───────────

THE NON-REALIST INTERPRETATION OF CHRISTIAN DOCTRINE*
Cupitt in the early 1980s — Stage 2

CHRISTIAN DOCTRINE	REALIST INTERPRETATION (Traditional; dogmatic)	NON-REALIST INTERPRETATION (Existential; ethical)
Creation	God as First Cause of the world; God causes the "Big Bang"...	Life should be treated as pure gift.
Providence	God preordains and supervises the entire course of world-events and of each life.	I believe that I will come through; my faith will not let me down.
Prayer	One seeks favor from a god-father.	Intercessory prayer as an expression of love and concern, and as a way of supporting the one prayed for. Prayer as attention to be-ing.
Incarnation	The metaphysical Son of God takes a human life as his own and becomes its subject.	Jesus is seen as embodying the religious ideal; he is Love in human form.
Resurrection	Jesus rises bodily from the tomb.	The believer who identifies himself with Jesus and dies with him in baptism rises to live a new, risen life.
Ascension	Jesus goes bodily up to Heaven in the sky.	The believer salutes Jesus as "Lord" in his life.
Eternal life	Post-mortem life in Heaven.	The "solar" living of the believer. She is no longer afraid of death.

* Cupitt often uses this diagram as a "teaching aid" to explain to students his non-realism of the early 1980s. Normally students reply: "Why can't we have a bit of both realism and non-realism?" Cupitt responds: "How can you?" and attempts to force them to choose.

truth, then how should people live? What kind of world is desirable when all we are left with is a beginningless, endless, and outsideless flux of conflicting human interpretations? What kind of societies can we create if there is nothing but our language and the meanings, truths, and interpretations that we have generated in using that language? What will be the result if we become the worldbuilders, continually making and remaking our own world? Can religion help in that re-creation when there is no-one or no thing "out-there" to give a blue-print as to how it must be?

Hence Cupitt, reinterpreting the Christian doctrine of *creatio ex nihilo*, wrote *Creation out of Nothing* and a string of books on how people might live "after God." This stage was also known as "active non-realism," as Cupitt attempted to show that to dispense with an objective God was not to unleash social anarchy or lack of moral codes. Rather, ethical responsibility or 'solar living' was high on his agenda. Indeed, instead of waiting to find the realm of God in another world, it must be created here. A world without God, contrary to much theological polemic, is not a world without value or ethics.

A slight deviation occurred as he changed tack to the philosopher Heidegger and the theme of ontology (be-ing) in stage 5. He argued that just as Heidegger tried to overcome the distinction between the Eternal realm (Being) and the temporal realm (becoming) by saying that only this world of be-ing (coming to be) existed, so we too must concentrate on how to live in this world of temporality (be-ing).

This brief discursus was succeeded by his fascination with Wittgenstein's proposal of a theological method that would ask, "What does ordinary language, as it is now used, tell us about people's picture of the world and their beliefs?" Accordingly, in stage 6 he attempted to work through the implications of the obvious fact that Western culture is no longer prescribed by the Church. It is still religious, but is it more of a Kingdom religiosity than an ecclesiastical religiosity? People still use religious language and discuss religious ideas, but they are less inclined to go to the churches to find answers to their questions. Furthermore, as religious authority weakens or becomes less relevant, religious language gets scattered across ordinary experience. The old religious words like "Heaven," "Hell," "Paradise," "Eden," "Bliss" remain in our common Parlance; we say, "She worships him, he idolizes her"; we talk about human love in religious language as we have for centuries. What might be termed a scattered or deconstructed religiousness is highly characteristic of the postmodern age, for the whole of life tends to take on a holy character. Thus, in a reflection of Wittgenstein's retreat from the academy,

Cupitt became convinced that ordinary language, rather than the traditional discourse of academic disciplines and church authorities, was "the best radical theologian."

In a trilogy of *Everyday Speech* books, he examined new idioms that had been established in common language. In the first book he showed how the word 'God' has come to be replaced by the word 'life.' Life had taken on all the attributes of a Divine Being. God was now demythologized into the contingent passing of life. In the second book Cupitt argued that everyday speech reveals that people think of themselves as surrounded by an "it" or "It All" which causes them to be apprehensive about life. He urged people to confront this fear and affirm their present lives. In the third book, *Kingdom Come in Everyday Speech*, he proposed that Kingdom religion had replaced ecclesiastical or Church religion. Ironically, he discovered, some elements of the secular, global world better suggest the Kingdom that Jesus envisaged than does the Church. Global organizations like the United Nations were dismantling tribalism and affirming humanitarian values so that the Kingdom was being realized without any help from a Church that could henceforth be consigned to the heritage industry. The message was clear: the Church needed to recover its relationship to the Kingdom.

By Kingdom religion Cupitt meant the kind of world to which the prophets and Jesus looked forward — the world of immediate experience, a world globalized, highly communicative and multi-ethnic. Thus Postmodernity was in many ways a somewhat secularized fulfillment of Biblical hope: it would prove more fruitful to view Christianity as an ongoing debate between ecclesiastical theology and Kingdom theology. Ecclesiastical theology was mediated and hierarchical, whereas Kingdom theology was immediate, non-hierarchical and egalitarian. The idea of the Kingdom was the Church's conscience and the Church needed to be criticized by it. The Kingdom was what Jesus had promised, the Church was what had evolved; and unfortunately history had shown that the Church is not quite as good as the Kingdom. Indeed, Cupitt suggested that the Church doesn't really want the Kingdom, preferring its own hierarchy, its mystery, authority and, above all, power.

All these themes have coalesced into the latest stage — the religion of the future. In another series of books Cupitt points to more democratic forms of religious belonging. The principal aim of religion should be therapeutic, helping people to overcome their reluctance to embrace this life and its transitoriness. Hence it is the Society of Friends (Quakers) and loose religious associations and networks that are creedless and Socratic that he looks to as forerunners of the "religion of the future." They have no ideology to peddle, but pose critical questions to those who claim to have ready answers. The new religious way of be-ing reflects the prevailing linguistic nihilism (*Philosophy's Own Religion*) that can transform traditional religion (*Reforming Christianity*), and there can be a synthesis of Eastern and Western thought (*Emptiness and Brightness*). Religion is not about seeking meaning in a metaphysical entity outside this world, but affirming this life (*Life, Life*). Religion is rooted in ordinary people's experience of life. The once great religious traditions are coming to an end, and people must learn to embrace a world of endless change and exchange. Our world is transient and lacks any guiding force from beyond. People must not seek after another Buddha, Jesus or guru, but look to themselves to create meaning (which is ever changing) and embrace the world as it is, unsupported and contingent.

At the heart of Cupitt's enterprise has been Friedrich Nietzsche's philosophy of attempting a drastic revaluation of everything. However, in this latest stage he combines Nietzsche with the thoughts of the Buddhist scholar, Nagajurna, emphasising that people best attain enlightenment when instead of relying on gurus, saints, or traditions, they create meaning themselves. Cupitt argues that having received its initial impulse two thousand years ago, Christianity is now running out of steam because people have rejected its authority. Mere reformation will not suffice; it needs new religious thought. Cupitt urges everyone to apply himself or herself to this task, but warns that it will not be accomplished by embracing "New Age" cults, many of which repeat past failures by insisting on Teachers and a 'spiritual' world apart from this one. Rather, new religious thought must emerge by "unlearning," or letting go of everything from previous generations. One must pass through the fires of nihilism into a radical humanism that repudiates any division between "Us" and "Them" and accepts this life and this world as the only ones.

Of course, Cupitt has not escaped criticism in any of these stages of his faith journey. His detractors are many. It is my chief aim in this book to counter those opponents who argue that his writings are flawed because without belief in an objective God, one cannot create a meaningful system of ethics or religion. I will argue that his ideas do resonate with ordinary people and show that his following extends to many parts of the globe. The "Cupitt phenomenon" is hardly limited to the solitary thoughts of an out-of-touch Cambridge don living in an academic ivory tower. On the contrary, whole networks of people (for example, Sea of Faith, the Jesus Seminar and the SnowStar Institute) study and debate the ideas proclaimed in his writings.

Cupitt has declined the invitation to write his own autobiography, insisting many times that his writings *are* his autobiography because they reflect a string of selves that have grappled with an *ever-changing* religious faith. By analyzing his writings in the context of a sketch of his life, I will provide insights into the way he has come to grips with being "godlessly religious." By so doing, I hope to rescue this prophetic voice from the "deafening silence" of the academic theological world and, more importantly, encourage many people to *dare* to open his books, and without fear and trembling read them!

Two major attempts have been made to analyse Cupitt's writings. Scott Cowdell's *Atheist Priest?* remains the standard textbook by which to evaluate his work, but is now many years out-of-date. Cupitt has averaged two books a years since 1988 and an enormous shift in his thinking has occurred. Stephen Ross White argued in *Don Cupitt and the Future of Christian Doctrine* (1994) that Cupitt's writings were an objection to and a movement away from "Christian orthodoxy" to the ahistorical position of being "purely religious." White defends belief in a real God and a real world against Cupitt's non-realism and anti-realism.

White's study was supposed to evaluate Cupitt's writings up to *After All* (1994), but although that book appears in White's bibliography it is nowhere mentioned in the text. Likewise, there is no evidence of an engagement with Cupitt's idea of "post-Christianity" which surfaces with the publication of that book. Rather, White's work encompasses Cupitt's thought only as far as *What Is a Story?* (1992). Moreover, despite White's explicit claim in Part 1 of the book that he is not attempting to refute Cupitt, he turns in Part 2 to do exactly that. White asserts that to remain within Christian orthodoxy one must, at the very least, adopt "critical realism." This is the theological position that, despite acknowledging the inadequacy of any human description of God, it is possible to reformulate a credible and morally acceptable objective content for belief in God. Beyond all our criticism and revisioning of Christian beliefs, it holds, there exist a Divine Being and a transcendent Truth, and the activity of God can be experienced and expressed in meaningful ways that are consonant with the latest scientific and epistemological theories. Cupitt, in replacing objectivity in religion with a postmodern spirituality that centres on human subjectivity, is damned.

It is obvious that White has not grasped the essence of Cupitt's radical agenda, but has set up a straw man (as, ironically, many accuse Cupitt himself of doing). Cowdell's more balanced approach captures the "spirit" of Cupitt, but in the last decade or so Cupitt has gone well beyond Cowdell's evaluation of him as an "Anglican apologist" and White's assessment that Cupitt has taken leave of the wrong conception of God.

He is now "post-Christian," more in tune with left-wing Quakerism and democratic religious thought. For him there is no objective God and no objective Truth.

In this book I will outline the stages of Cupitt's writings in dialogue with these two authors as well as a host of commentators whom one can list under the broad rubric of "refuters." Moreover, I will show that his critics err in setting Cupitt over against "critical realism," which ultimately involves playing a *different* religious game. As Colin Crowder points out:

> What is needed . . . is a detailed study of Cupitt's way of working, of the rhetorical structuring of his radical vision. It will not suffice to profess confidence in a "qualified theological realism" (or Macquarrie's "existential-ontological theism"), as Cowdell does. . . . A substantial critique of Cupitt . . . would have to consider the implications of a radically anthropocentric constructivism.[2]

Crowder hoped that Cowdell would attempt that "detailed study," for he considered that *Atheist Priest?* was too brief an analysis of Cupitt's writings. When Cowdell failed to oblige, preferring to concentrate on Christology in his *Is Jesus Unique?* (1996), Crowder published *God and Reality* (1997), which was a symposium of views (both for and against) on non-realism. It is the purpose of this book to provide that detailed study of "Cupitt's way of working" and "his radical vision." In a forthcoming book I will show what kind of religious faith is possible without an objective God, and evaluate what Cupitt proposes as a faith for the future that centres solely on the creativity of human beings.

In conclusion, this present book sets out to demonstrate that Cupitt's writings are too important to be dismissed as offbeat or objectionable, and that they are of great significance in enabling many people to create a "faith for the future." Rather than be a destroyer of anyone's faith, it is my aim to defend Cupitt as one who has allowed people to find freedom from the many forms of realism that have long kept them in oppression. Cupitt's writings are a form of liberation, not enslavement, and of incalculable benefit to those who wish to find a faith that is consistent with a world cut adrift from the moorings of realism — and of which we are the creators.

So how did it all begin?

The Formative Years

Don Cupitt was born on 22nd May, 1934 at a "Maternity Home" (as such places were then called) in the industrial textile town of Oldham, Lancashire, England. He was the eldest of four children born to Robert and Norah Cupitt. Norah Cupitt (1913–1997), a local girl, was the daughter of John Gregson, a butcher. She had worked at a sewing machine in a clothing factory for two or three years, but after marrying at the age of 20 did not work outside the home. Robert Cupitt (1911–1992) is described on Don's birth certificate as a "gas engineer." His father, Bertram Cupitt, was a plumber who had served in the Royal Engineers throughout the First World War. The family originated in Derbyshire and Nottinghamshire, where a number remained; but some migrated overseas. At least one settled in the United States, where the name is still found in Philadelphia and Texas. Another, Ostin Cupitt, was an early free settler in Australia (1797). Here the name still remains fairly common, for example in Brisbane, where Don Cupitt's enemies report with glee the existence of a business named: "CUPITT DEMOLITIONS."

Don's paternal grandmother was Emma Hester Cupitt, née Wayman, the eldest daughter of a large Nottingham family. As a girl, she had won a place in the local Medical School, but had been obliged to reject it — as was the case with many Victorian girls for whom duty to family came first — in order to help care for the younger children. As a result of this harsh disappointment, she developed a lifelong fascination for occult and exotic knowledge: gnosticism, theosophy, divination by dreams, tea leaves, tarot cards, palmistry and mediumship, and the study of Eastern religions. Even as a child Cupitt was skeptical of his grandmother's interest in such things, but he seems to have caught her passionate hunger for knowledge and an understanding of the consolation to be found in the world of ideas — precious gifts that he has never lost.

Emma's son, Robert Cupitt, or "Bob" as he was always called, was short and stocky, with black hair. He was good-looking and athletic. His exceptional driving energy must readily have attracted attention, for while yet in his early twenties, he was in charge of a large gang of men who installed gas mains running across farmland outside Oldham. Later, he tried to improve his lot by enrolling in what was known locally as "Night School" (a forerunner of Further Education Colleges) and qualified as a heating and ventilating engineer. Since this involved the fabrication of sheet-metal ducting, beginning in 1939 he was assigned to spend the early years of the Second World War establishing factories and training workers to manufacture wings and fuselages for fighter aircraft. Later, he built military landing craft. Although the pace of work was furious and the family had to move every few months, at least he remained at home. The family survived both the bombing of the industrial Midlands in 1940 and of London by the V1s and V2s in 1944.

Established now as a successful manager and a "rising man," who had moved a few rungs up the social ladder of class-conscious Britain, Bob Cupitt decided that his children should be educated privately. After attending preparatory schools, the boys were sent on to Charterhouse, and the girls to Cheltenham Ladies College. The names of the schools will speak volumes to English readers about the social ambition of the Cupitts, and their bold determination in undertaking to educate four children at leading British boarding schools out of post-tax income alone.

The Charterhouse that Don encountered in the years just after World War II (1947–1952) has been well described by the novelist Simon Raven in his *Shadows on the Grass*. Founded on the site of a Carthusian monastery in Smithfield, London in 1611, Charterhouse typified the English "Public" (Private) School tradition of the union of Establishment culture with Established religion. In 1873 it moved to a two hundred acre site in Godalming, Surrey, and in 1927 its Victorian buildings were dominated by a Chapel of such a size that it could accommodate every boy in the School. Its architect, Sir Giles Gilbert Scott, designed it to be the largest War memorial in England. Here it was that Cupitt came under the influence of the Established Church, and his love-hate affair with the Church of England has lasted to this very day.

Like many other boys at the age of thirteen or so, he was duly prepared for the Anglican rite of Confirmation. Although for some of the students this was just another rite of passage that had to be endured, Cupitt took seriously his tutelage by the distinguished Early Church historian Henry Bettenson, whose theological position he subsequently described as "Designer realism." In this variation on the Argument from Design put forward by Thomas Aquinas and William Paley, the existence of God can be inferred from the good design of the cosmos. "Where there is a Plan, there must be a Planner," Cupitt was told. Although it made God rather remote (and was subject to the danger of deism), this doctrinal system nicely suited an English educational system whose goal was to inspire students to seek God in all areas of knowledge from biology to art. True, the underlying Platonism would mean that God was always out of reach, but by one's best endeavours and diligent work one could glimpse something of the Divine. Yet, even at this early age Cupitt was not entirely convinced. Two incidents from this time show that he was not one to accept uncritically what he was told.

The first was his deep suspicion of a Christian tradition that mixed nationalism with religious values. He began to question the dominant symbol of Charterhouse — the Chapel — built in remembrance of the 700 Carthusians (former pupils at Charterhouse) who had died in the First World War. The shape of the High Altar was echoed by a soldier's coffin that was suspended some meters above it, and much was made of such texts as: "Greater love hath no man than this, that he lay down his life for his friends" (John 15:13). This intermingling of military, political and religious values disturbed him; for he intuited that to see Christ's death on the cross as somehow justifying the sacrifice of young lives was wrong. The faith he was being taught made him very uncomfortable.

Second, Charterhouse introduced him to two other great systems of thought — Platonism and Darwinism. During his last year there, Cupitt and other specially selected school monitors (prefects) attended weekly sessions in the Headmaster's study, during which they read Plato's *Republic* aloud. He describes the experience as "all very Victorian": being inculcated to participate in an Imperial ruling class that demanded an often paternalistic and even patronizing ethic of service to others. It was doing unto others "for their own good" and the greater good of the Empire!

Cupitt, who already knew himself to be of an unusually reflective disposition, responded strongly to Plato. And Platonism, of course, could be intertwined with Christian theology quite easily, reinforcing the notion of a distinction between this world of mere appearances and a truer world elsewhere. But Darwinism was a different matter. Simply put, it was a threat to Christian faith. If Darwin was correct, one need not postulate a divine creator to account for human origins. Although Cupitt was not ready to rebel against his Confirmation vows, his Christian faith was left hanging by a thread.[1]

Charterhouse proved to be a good investment for Bob Cupitt. His son, obviously highly gifted academically, prospered under a talented array of "Masters." Thus he learnt Botany from the notable field botanist of the Himalayas, Oleg Polunin; English from W.C. Sellar, co-author of *1066 and All That*; Italian from the poet-mountaineer Wilfred Noyce; and Art from Ian Fleming-Williams. The legacy of Charterhouse was that Cupitt left it much affected by Platonism and Darwinism, and unsettled by Christianity. These three themes were to be crucial for his future development and still underlie much of his writings.

In 1952 Cupitt won an Exhibition to go up to Cambridge University for undergraduate study and in October of that year he began to read Natural Sciences at Trinity Hall. Most students find their University days to be a time of emotional upheaval, unsettled by academic, social, and religious anxieties, and Cupitt was no exception. Not only that, but since his home background was completely secular — neither of his parents ever having taken him to Church or discussed religion — his three years at Cambridge must have been equally perplexing and worrisome to Bob and Norah.

On almost his first Sunday at Cambridge Cupitt was converted again, this time to Evangelical Christianity ("Doctrinal Realism") with a rigid emphasis on "knowing the Lord." Today he is at a loss to explain what he now calls "this aberration." Perhaps this form of Christianity offered to an apprehensive "freshman" the security of membership in a strong, cohesive group. For a while he enjoyed vivid religious experiences, but they faded as he became aware of the intellectual emptiness of evangelicalism. Ever the freethinker, he was affronted by what he saw as the psychological tyranny that the leadership wielded over its members, and he quickly gave up that form of Christianity.

During his second year, still studying Natural Sciences, he began work on a paper examining the History and Philosophy of Science — then a rather new subject — while at the same time energetically pursuing the study of the conservative and liberal theologians of the period. He was also reading mystics and existentialists. It was at this point that he flirted with a form of Protestant ethical idealism made popular from the twenties through the forties by the liberal Anglican Dean of St. Paul's Cathedral, the Very Reverend William Ralph Inge. Dean Inge stood in the line of figures like Tolstoy and Schweitzer who interpreted Christianity as high ethical living, a "reverence for life." His catchphrase, "Christianity is a divine life, not a divine science," attracted many to the Modern Churchmen's Union, where liberal Christian views on doctrines and ethics were aired.

However, whilst the emphasis on ethical living was later to make a significant reappearance in Cupitt's thought, it was Inge's attraction to the mystics that interested him most of all in his Cambridge days. For Inge, mysticism was the one essential ingredient of all religions. Simply put, it was an ascent into knowledge of the divine, and a path that anyone could travel. He often quoted the Egyptian-born neo-Platonist philosopher, Plotinus (204–270 C.E.) to the effect that the only thing required for the apprehension of divine truth is a faculty "which we all possess, but few use." Cupitt's faith journey led to mysticism and what he later labelled "Ladder Realism." In view of the Platonic insistence on God as the First Principle of all things, the way to find God was a quasi-ascetic and contemplative path. By overcoming the distance between the Divine and yourself, mysticism allowed you to "climb the ladder," pushing out of the way the obstacles that blocked a direct apprehension of God. The rungs of the ladder (meditation, contemplation, rapture, and ecstasy) would lead after much dedication to mystical union. This insistence on following an ascetical or purgative path reappears many times in Cupitt's writings.

Now intensely religious, he did what no Cupitt had done before. Much to the surprise and obvious dismay of his parents, who were concerned about the low income and status of the clergy, he decided for ordination in the Anglican Church. In his third year he turned from Natural Science to study Theology under the direction of the distinguished church historian Owen Chadwick. He tried to cram too much into a one-year course; and although the result would have been highly gratifying for most students, he was disappointed to be awarded only an Upper Second Class degree.

Like many others of his age in post-War Britain Cupitt had taken the option of deferring the mandatory two years' National (Military) Service until after his first degree, in the hope that by 1955 it might be abolished. Unfortunately, for him, it was not. In view of his scientific studies, he was assigned to the Royal Signals, commissioned, and posted out to Cyprus in charge of a signal troop attached to an Artillery regiment. He managed to include a number of standard philosophy books in his troop's equipment, and spent an otherwise dull time reading them at Coral Bay, near Ktima.

After the Army it was back to Cambridge in October 1957 to train for the priesthood. He entered a well-known Anglican Theological College, Westcott House, which was seen as the traditional nursery of liberal bishops. His first year (1957/1958) was spent on an intensive postgraduate course in the Philosophy of Religion. This had to be done via Trinity Hall, where Robert Runcie (a future Archbishop of Canterbury) had succeeded Owen Chadwick as Dean. It was in this field that Cupitt found his vocation and, despite a severe bout of flu on the examination days, was at last able to gain a First Class degree. The possibility, indeed the likelihood of an academic career suddenly seemed to open. Moreover, K.M. Carey, the Principal of Westcott House, extracted a promise that Cupitt would, if and when called upon, return to Westcott House and succeed John Habgood (a future Archbishop of York) as Vice-Principal.

Cupitt was ordained on Trinity Sunday 1959 and for his curacy chose to return to his roots in working class industrial Lancashire, with the idea of finding a way to bridge the wide gap between his origins and what his education had made of him. Here he served from 1959 to 1962 — an era associated with radical theologians and much theological angst among inner-city priests in America and Britain, who wondered how best to communicate a two thousand year old Gospel to an increasingly "secularized," urban population. Although the writings of Harvey Cox (*The Secular City*), Paul van Buren (*The Secular Meaning of the Gospel*) and John A. T. Robinson (*Honest to God*) were still to be published, their work constituted an undeniable context for the situation in which he found himself. Ministering to a parish in inner-city Salford raised the same issues that these writers were addressing. In particular, Cupitt admits almost two decades later to the religious difficulties that he faced in having to endorse supernatural explanations of the medical problems of patients in the local hospital. How could he repeat the prescribed prayers from the Anglican *Book of Common Prayer*? How could he tell a man dying of cancer that this devastating sickness had been sent by God? Could he bite his tongue and agree that the birth of a handicapped child was a sign of God's displeasure, or should he insist on a secular medical interpretation? On many occasions, Cupitt reports, he summoned up the courage to offer the "natural causes" explanations. He admits, however, that at the time he "did not fully work out the implications of what (he) was saying," and inner conflicts lay dormant that would surface with a vengeance at a later date.[2]

At the same time the Diocese of Manchester required him to remain academically active by writing theological essays. John Heywood Thomas, a philosopher of religion on the staff of Manchester University, was assigned as his supervisor. From this period stem some of Cupitt's earliest published writings. In his philosophy he was still broadly Neo-Thomist, affirming the One who is the *ens realissimum* (the most real entity) beyond all human images that we use to describe God. However, at the same time he was busily trying to assimilate the work of Kant, Kierkegaard and Bultmann, a curriculum that would in the end aid him in deconstructing the unhelpful images of the Divine Being and lead at last to more liberal views.

In 1962 Cupitt's three-year curacy expired, and he duly returned to Westcott House to succeed John Habgood. Life there during term-time was extremely busy, but the vacations proved unbearably lonely for a bachelor who had lived in all-male residential institutions for nearly twenty years, and had been kept too busy to think about the opposite sex. At about this time he was taken aside one day by his supervisor, G. F. Woods, a small precise Lancastrian who, though himself unmarried, offered him a solemn warning: "Don't let them keep you so busy that you forget to get married." After some thought he remembered a friend from his National Service, Roger Day, whose family home in the Chilterns was near to where the Cupitt family then lived, and with whose blonde sister Susan he had occasionally exchanged glances. Events moved rapidly, and he and Susan married in December 1963. He describes his marriage as "almost his only piece of quite unmixed good fortune." They moved into a Victorian terraced house in Collier Road, Cambridge, and children began to arrive almost immediately. They had no capital wealth, and lived in a tied cottage on 810 English pounds per annum, but in those days "personal finance" had not been invented, and they were content in the knowledge that the Church was looking after them. In 1965 he was offered the post of Dean of Emmanuel College, with a fellowship and the task of directing studies in Theology. Three years later came his first University teaching appointment, an Assistant Lectureship in the Philosophy of Religion, with a three-year tenure of the Stanton Lectureship added for good measure. He threw himself energetically into the work of the Faculty of Divinity.

Thus in the 1960s and early 1970s Cupitt was still in high favor. His first books had appeared, gaining the imprimatur even of respected liberal scholars. Indeed, his only really controversial stand until 1967 was to abandon literal belief in the Devil, a position he took to protect "monotheism against the enslavement of men (*sic*) by superstitious fear."[3] Cupitt argued that the eradication of belief in Satan would set people free to worship the loving and compassionate God whom Jesus came to reveal.

Cupitt was part of a Church of England that at the time was marked by optimism, a projected membership growth, and an expectation of the rising quantity of ordained clergy that would be needed to cope with the demand. He wrote articles for *The Listener* that were tolerably well received, despite one reader who responded to his sharp critique of the charismatic movement by declaring that she was praying for his conversion. He seemed surely destined for a distinguished career within the Established Church.

Then, while writing *The Leap of Reason*, he experienced a few weeks of great intellectual excitement, and realized that whatever happened he must (as he puts it) "specialize on the creative side." Two snap decisions illustrate the point. First, when he was suddenly offered an ecclesiastical appointment that was a traditional path to the highest office, he rejected it without hesitation or subsequent regret. Second, when he was asked to join a radical group of scholars who were discussing what was to become the most controversial book of the 1970s — *The Myth of God Incarnate* (1977) — he promptly accepted. The die was cast, and soon he was being described in print as "a fallen angel." Some will say that he lacked the essential virtue of prudence, but he would reply that he had glimpsed and briefly tasted something more fatally alluring than anything else in the world — something for which one must risk everything . . .

The Negative Theology

1967–1979

Christ and the Hiddenness of God (1971)
The Leap of Reason (1976)

As I have indicated, Cupitt has not always been a radical Christian. Indeed, for a short time, he was a theological conservative, even flirting during his undergraduate years with the evangelical Christian Union. However, from 1967–1979 he moved from Protestant evangelicalism to a more and more liberal Christian outlook. This development was spurred by his reading of the mystics, which led him to embrace the negative or *apophatic* tradition, in which God is deemed unknowable and ineffable. His main task during those years was to "move from grossly inadequate to less inadequate images of God" so that "the trail of broken images would become an arrow pointing towards the transcendent."[1] Thus an objective God was still real and meaningful to him. Although He might be viewed only "as in a mirror dimly," there was nonetheless a controlling Divine Being "out there" who undergirded the Universe. Cupitt accepted the view of Platonic Christianity that beyond our world of appearances existed a "real world" and a "real God," and that our lives are moving towards another more glorious home which we enter through death.

In 1971 he produced his first book, *Christ and the Hiddenness of God*. He argued that since God is ultimate mystery, it is only by focusing on Jesus that we can glimpse something of God. Because he is the model of faith, people must look to the Jesus of the past as the key to their relationship with God. Jesus shows people what it means to proclaim and to live as though God were near, even while recognizing the paradoxical fact that God is remote, sublime, and incomprehensible. His cry from the cross, "My God, my God, why have you forsaken me?" (Mark 15:34 // Matt. 27:47), is one all Christians will have to utter.

This perspective on understanding Jesus set the tone for Cupitt's negative theology. Immersed in the apophatic tradition he declared that one could never achieve total knowledge of God. Therefore one must refer to that reality only analogically through the work and person of Jesus. In a hint of the next step in his abandonment of all analogies (and an objective God) Cupitt wrote:

> the classical negative theology cannot succeed by itself in making a clear assertion about God. But we should not leave it for the moment without pointing out that the mystic rejoices in this situation. His message is that theism and atheism are indiscriminable: that is precisely the point he tries to make in speaking about God as Silence, a Void, an Abyss, a Desert, Night, a Shoreless Sea. His journey is a journey into unknowing. At least one very important strand in religious aspiration would prefer to say that God is nothing rather than that he is anything, because atheism is nearer the mark than even the most refined analogical theism.[2]

It is remarkable how many of the themes that will occupy Cupitt in the succeeding years appear here. He is not ready at this stage to abandon the objectivity of faith, and still argues that religious statements make some cognitive claims about the reality of nature and God. Religious language can connect with that Ultimate reality about which it purports to speak.

This subject is further explored five years later in *The Leap of Reason*. Cupitt's commitment to realism and objectivism makes him insist upon the cognitive nature of religious statements and to reject the non-realism that he later came to advocate. He asserts that a person's religious search begins with a pre-linguistic religious experience from which arises a conviction of the possibility of an objective, transcendent Divine Being who is in some sense "outside" this world. This conviction, resulting from the person's own "heightened consciousness" Cupitt calls "the leap of reason." Adapting Plato's parable of the cave in *The Republic* (Book 6, Part 7), he asserts that by a leap of reason one can think of an "outside world." Unlike Plato, whose cave has an open entrance, allowing an exterior fire to cause the prisoners within to cast shadows on one of its walls and thus learn of another world outside, Cupitt asks us to imagine a cave without any opening and from which the prisoner has never left. For this person there is no *reason* to suppose the existence of an outside world. His cave is "a closed and self-maintaining physical system." Yet, suddenly one day the prisoner imagines that there might be another world "outside" or "beyond." It is a difficult "mental act," a heightened consciousness, accompanied by doubts and fears. Yet it still remains — a leap of reason that allows him to think that his world is bounded, that it has another world beyond it. The prisoner has no proof that this other world exists and can only describe to others his heightened consciousness, his leap of reason.

This heightened consciousness or leap of reason is the spiritual state in which many Christians finds themselves. A heightened consciousness allows one to glimpse the transcendent deity who is "beyond" or "outside" our world. Communities of faith are those who have experienced this heightened consciousness and express this religious experience in a religious system that includes myth, ritual, doctrine etc. However, this system must itself be negated, for the great monotheistic religions have always stressed that unless the difference between a religious system and the Object of worship is maintained, idolatry will result. This creates an inherent agnosticism that can be overcome only by both affirming and denying all religious symbols. Accordingly, Cupitt likens religion to a "fiery dance" in which adherents avow both the presence and absence of God.

In the 1970s, then, Cupitt sees the individual experiencing God by a prelinguistic "heightened consciousness" that results in a leap of reason. Yet at the same time, God is also strangely hidden. And although Cupitt writes out of the Christian tradition, he is much concerned to recognise the pluralistic faith situation that is found in the United Kingdom. Post-War Britain has gradually become a multi-cultural, multi-racial and multi-faith society, a fact that Christian theologians need to take note of. Interestingly, Cupitt views ethics as separating theistic from non-theistic religions. In theistic religions the person of faith glimpses a possibility of the moral transcendent. Hence, the transcendent must be good and personal, and must include an objective God who by grace bestows positive personal moral qualities on the believer. In non-theistic religion (Cupitt here mentions Buddhism) ethics does not reveal the nature of the transcendent, and so is replaced by a non-personal "self-negating ethic" that produces an inactive asceticism. (Ironically, in the light of what is to come from Cupitt, his emphasis upon transcendence works against relativism!) A pluralistic society does not have to drift towards relativism or subjectivism. Rather, theistic religions, with their emphasis upon the possibility of transcendence, can overcome it. The great theistic religious teachers are consciousness-raisers; and it is by a heightened consciousness (the leap of reason) that relativism is transcended and pluralism embraced. This stance places him squarely in the liberal Protestant ethical tradition, and solidly in the context of the major theistic world faiths, all of which point to the one unseen transcendent universal deity.

Cupitt's other major preoccupations during this stage are an engagement with issues relating to the conceptual gap between the Jesus of history and Christ of faith, and critical Christian ethics. It is noteworthy that three who presently rank among Cupitt's principal "refuters" would be content had he continued to espouse the beliefs he then held. David L. Edwards has endorsed Cupitt's views in *Christ and the Hiddenness of God*. Similarly, Anthony Thiselton considers *The Leap of Reason* his best book, and Stephen Ross White admits that Cupitt's position of devout agnosticism was close to that of many of the Church Fathers and the mediaeval mystics. In short, Cupitt at this time was well within the orthodox Christian fold.

So what turned a theologian of the negative and mystical tradition, one who might have remained a liberal but conforming academic, into a feared radical whose books would shake the foundations of orthodoxy? What was there in the "early" Cupitt that impelled him at last to affirm the Death of God and the end of metaphysics? What brought about the change that led an admirer like Edwards, who in 1971 affirmed that Cupitt was "a very clever man who believes in God through Christ," to demand in 1989 that he resign his priesthood?

Commentators look primarily to one philosopher to account for Cupitt's move from liberalism to non-realism. Rowan Williams, whilst also giving the teachings of the Buddha some weight, puts the principal blame on to the shoulders of Immanuel Kant. Likewise Gavin Hyman views Kant as the culprit, arguing that Cupitt moved from Kant's universalism to a more subjectivist relativism by advocating cultural-relative categories instead of universal categories. Once the transcendent realm was no longer necessary, the noumenal was abandoned in favour of phenomena: with no Real world "out there" all that remains is this world of phenomena. Hyman also identifies Kant as the person responsible for Cupitt's interest in negative theology and disinterestedness, and the main contributor towards the subversion into non-realism.[3] To be sure, Kant played a major role in Cupitt's move to non-realism, but two other equally important factors are overlooked by Cupitt's detractors.

The first is his acceptance of Charles Darwin's evolutionary theory with its implications of a contingent world:

> Darwinism . . . still remains the most wonderful and potent
> demonstration of the sheer power of purely 'immanent' and grad-

ualistic or naturalistic explanation. . . . Although Darwinism is, as some people like to insist, 'only a scientific theory,' its implications are formidable. If Darwin is right, there seems no need to postulate any special divine action in order to account for the first appearance, and the capacities, of human beings in the world. But Darwin obviously is right on the main issue. Has he not then made God redundant?[4]

Faced with the insight that human beings are "just talking animals" without a soul, and having no need of another world "out there," he could now jettison what he had first encountered as a pupil at Charterhouse — the Platonic assertion of a more real world beyond this one. What mattered was *this* world, for there was no metaphysical world elsewhere. What was needed was a religion that would help people live in the here-and-now and not hanker after somewhere else that obviously does not exist.

Closely related to the repudiation of another reality was the recognition that a Creator had become a superfluous assumption. Darwin's naturalistic explanation had dispensed with belief in Someone or Something guiding and sustaining the Universe. Chance, time, and natural processes accounted for the random and yet complex state of affairs that we find. Cupitt confesses that though philosophers don't usually admit the profound impact of scientific theories, he knows that for him, Darwin "has been the chief influence in bringing about the Death of God and the end of metaphysics."[5] Darwinism, which he also learned at Charterhouse and whose implications for theology had unsettled him, also led at last to Nothing (No Thing).

Secondly, Cupitt's philosophical reading at Cambridge prompted a shift in thinking from British-style logical empiricism, which relied on realist notions of Truth, to the challenge of post-Kantianism, Nietzsche and the French postmodernists such as Derrida, who were tilting towards ideas of multiple truths (anti-realism). Before he could adopt anti-realism philosophically, he first had to declare that he was anti-realist theologically. This position he termed "non-realism." Unfortunately, the terms anti-realism and non-realism are often blurred and conflated by his critics. Strictly-speaking, anti-realism is the philosophical viewpoint opposed to realism. Non-realism tends to be used in the *religious* context, upholding the view that God lacks objective existence. So, one can be a non-realist in religion without being anti-realist philosophically, as in the case of the *Sea of Faith* writer Graham Shaw or the philosopher Iris Murdoch. Conversely, philosophical anti-realists like Anglican Bishops John Shelby

Spong and Richard Holloway can be realists in theology. Cupitt is **both** anti-realist and non-realist. Originally, the term "non-realism" derives from Hilary Putnam, who used it to describe a philosophical position between Realism and Idealism. Cupitt admits that he once thought he had invented the term, but his use is obviously different from Putnam's.[6]

In 1980, however, to declare oneself a non-realist was not a simple or a painless undertaking, but a very costly "coming out" that marked Cupitt for the rest of his University career as "deviant" or "unsound". For an academic theologian who is also an ordained minister of religion to declare that the objectivity of God is redundant is something like a garage mechanic's verdict that an engine can't be fixed. Like the distressed motorist who angrily demands that the mechanic be sacked, the theological and ecclesiastical worlds reacted with alacrity.

Stage 2

Non-realism–
"coming out"
1980–1985

Taking Leave of God (1980)

When *Taking Leave of God* appeared there was a hell of a
row and I realized that it had finished my career as an academic
and in the Church. In some ways *Taking Leave of God* was the
culmination of the earlier books, but it was also the start for
everything that went on since. . . . It was known that I had
"come out" in a big way. The Cambridge system meant that I got
a University Assistant lectureship in 1968 and only got tenure
in 1976, by which time I was over forty. Then I was reasonably
safe. I couldn't actually be kicked out, so I started the disclosing
publications at the end of the 1970s.[1]

Cupitt's "coming out" into non-realism coincided, as he remarks,
with his gaining the "safety" of University tenure. Up until 1980 or thereabouts, Professors in Theology at Oxford and Cambridge Universities
were by and large Anglican clergymen. As a result, academic freedom of
thought was constrained by concerns of "theological orthodoxy," since
Faculty Chairs were given only to theologians who were "in good standing" with the Established Church. The professional pressure or unwritten
rule in Cupitt's workplace was that he should always be discreet, avoid
writing tendentious articles, and defend the (Anglican) Faith. The conflicting claims of allegiance to the Church and the University represent a
constant theme of Cupitt's life.[2] So to publish a book with the provocative title *Taking Leave of God* was a very risky venture for a scholarly clergyman.

It is important to note two strong hints suggesting that Cupitt himself was apprehensive about really "coming out." The first is that the orig-

inal title to the book was *The Autonomy of Religion*. This would certainly have been less provocative and might even have passed unnoticed. The appeal to autonomy bespeaks Cupitt's rejection of "dependency" in any form of religion; and his promotion of Buddhism as a religious way stems from that tradition's emphasis on independence of thought. Indeed, the central thrust of *Taking Leave of God* is to provide a moral critique of Christian faith as a heteronomous external control system. With his barbs aimed at the very religious system that would seek to bridle him, he describes his new religion as Christian Buddhism: "The content, the spirituality and the values, are Christian; the form is Buddhist."[3]

Second and at least equally important, in *Taking Leave of God* Cupitt does not expound a fully non-realist position. The opening quotation from Meister Eckhart that 'Man's highest parting occurs, when for God's sake, he takes leave of God' (Sermon: *Qui audit me*) is extremely (and deliberately) ambivalent. It can be interpreted either in a non-realist way or, perhaps preferably, in a mystical, onto-theological, realist way — as Jacques Derrida does in *Writing and Difference* where he can be read as admitting the existence of a transcendent deity.[4] Later, in *Mysticism after Modernity*, Cupitt challenges Derrida's interpretation of Meister Eckhart, arguing that Eckhart was in fact a thoroughgoing "non-realist." However, this was eighteen years **after** *Taking Leave of God* and it is obvious that in 1980 Cupitt was more than willing to leave an ambiguity (or escape-hatch for himself!) for a mystical reading of Meister Eckhart. This is confirmed by Cupitt's own admission that the book "has a hidden transcendent beyond objectivity," about which Cowdell expressed "great surprise."[5] Indeed, a close inspection of *Taking Leave of* God clearly reveals a mystical or even agnostic Kantian position:

> The most we can say is that it is religiously appropriate to think that there may be beyond the God of religion a transcendent divine mystery witnessed to in various ways by the faiths of mankind. But we cannot say anything about it.[6]

At the time Eric James was the nearest to understanding Cupitt's standpoint. He noted in a book review in *The Times* in 1981, that that it was absurd to accuse a man of 'atheism' who could write: "My God is still the *deus absconditus*, the hidden God who is found at last to hide himself in the depths of the heart." Cupitt adopts a theocentric pluralist position close to that of theologian John Hick in his book, *God Has Many Names* (1980) — a stance that draws support from the major religious faiths whose various religious expressions witness to belief in a Divine Being.

However, as Cupitt himself noted in his own review of *God Has Many Names*, it is a position akin to "thin-line theism." Once you begin to admit that religion is human and varied and that everything said about God is inconsistent, symbolic, and culturally conditioned, then why not take the next step? This is to admit that God and religion are human constructs, and that talk about God is a cultural expression rather than a metaphysical description. Although Hick was not prepared to take that step and would propound and repeat the same system of thought for the whole of his academic life, Cupitt was soon to do so. However, it would be correct to concur with Cupitt himself, as he observes in a preface to a second impression of *Taking Leave of God*, "that when the dust settles it may be seen that the early charges of 'atheism' were over-simple."

The emphasis on negative theology leads Cupitt to bring together three lines of thought — internalization, autonomy, and disinterestedness. Belief in supernatural doctrines is replaced by a self-chosen way of "living religiously" that helps people find meaning and solace despite the vicissitudes of their existence. In language almost redolent of liberation theologians, orthodoxy (right belief) is replaced by orthopraxis (right conduct). "God" becomes a guiding spiritual ideal internal to the self. Cupitt acknowledges his debt to Kant, Hegel, Meister Eckhart and Kierkegaard, and ends up with an inner spirituality that consists of "internalized *a priori* principles, freely adopted and self-imposed" which he calls "the religious requirement." In 1980 Cupitt is still influenced by the Enlightenment Project and the active, heroic, self of modernity. He promotes a highly individualistic spirituality tinged with Nietzschean heroism that looks to the self to create new religious values. It will be another six years before Cupitt rejects the autonomous hero of Modernism in favour of postmodern ideas of the decentered self. Finally in 1998 he was prepared to admit that the "autonomous self" was perhaps too optimistic a project:

> As a proposed solution to the problem of religious happiness, *Taking Leave of God* asks too much of the self, makes the self too big, lays too great a burden upon the self. Even its author no longer wants to be and is no longer able to be the person the book asks him to be.[7]

The important point here, one that will be reiterated throughout this book, is that Cupitt is always "in movement." This leads him to an espousal of non-realism because the "fixed position" of realism is its opposite. The catchphrases for Cupitt become: "the truth is in the movement" and "meanings don't stay still for long enough."

Taking Leave of God thrust Cupitt into controversy. Indeed, one reviewer described it as "a knuckle-duster" of a book that would deliver many deadly blows. Robert Runcie (his former Tutor at Trinity Hall and in 1980 the Archbishop of Canterbury) criticized him in a sermon preached at Little Saint Mary's Church, Cambridge, just after the publication of the book. This was reported in the *Cambridge Evening News* and made sensational reading. Runcie sent Cupitt a private note of (qualified) apology afterwards, and declined to elaborate for the national press. The debate raged and the battle lines were drawn in newspaper articles, church periodicals, and on radio programs. The newly appointed F. D. Maurice Professor at King's College, London, Keith Ward, published an orthodox Christian reply, aptly titled *Holding Fast to God*, in which he criticised Cupitt for inappropriately portraying God as an arbitrary all-determining tyrant. If only Cupitt could understand God in a more benevolent way, then his insistence on human autonomy would be granted. The Christian God does not deny human autonomy, but seeks to bring the divine and human wills together in perfect obedience to a good and loving Creator who has been revealed in the life of Christ. As Ward saw it, Cupitt was simply talking about the wrong God!

If Ward and others had searched a bit more diligently, however, they would have found that Cupitt had not completely taken leave of a transcendent divine mystery. Rather, his central point was that adherence to belief in an objective God was insignificant compared with the task of finding a paradigm of religious expression by which modern people could live. It was left to his next book to explore further the implications of this insight for delineating a faith appropriate to autonomous modern people who had long since left supernaturalism behind.

The World to Come (1982)

The World to Come is one of Cupitt's most important writings, yet it usually receives only perfunctory consideration. It is dedicated to "those who have given him encouragement and support" against the "aggravation" caused by the publication of *Taking Leave of God*. He explores the implications of seeing Christianity as a practice-religion rather than a belief-religion. Readers are asked to disregard the risk of being described by others as "atheists," and to join Cupitt in "search of the faith of the age to come." This invitation is extended especially to those who are on the margins of the churches and who find them oppressive and intellectually bankrupt.

The "Hyperborean faith" (after the Hyperboreans of Greek Legend who discover a pleasant and sustaining environment beyond the north wind) is to be found by letting go of all the fixed points of realism and passing through nihilism and the void. There will be a crisis of faith, and like the Biblical injunction "one must lose one's faith in order to find it" on the far side of the nihil. The result will be a "social theology" of the "new order." In the spirit of Jesus' teaching we can work for a better world by disregarding self-interest and the will to power. Jesus was the prophet of a new religious revolution because he announced "the bankruptcy of the existing religious order" and "proclaimed the coming of a new order in which faith would be fully inward and autonomous." Cupitt thus opens the way for other radicals to join him in trying to create a new Christian faith.

Although Cowdell doubted that many would find Cupitt's Hyperborean brand of religion very satisfying, history has shown otherwise.[8] Indeed, Stewart Sutherland's estimation in *The Times Literary Supplement* that there is a "significant group of those within and beyond the boundaries of the churches who will buy, read and be stimulated by this book" was closer to the mark. Even in 1982, Cupitt was not a solitary prophet, but was writing radical theology because many others were of a like mind. Some of these "ordinary" radical Christians, who wrote sympathetic letters to Cupitt in 1980–1982, became the founding members of what in six years would emerge in the United Kingdom — and which now extends to many parts of the globe — as the Sea of Faith Network.

Both Thiselton and Cowdell correctly observe that Kant's influence has been replaced by that of Nietzsche. Cupitt's "coming out" has a parallel with Nietzsche's "God is dead" and "the new order." Thiselton is particularly perceptive in bringing out the implications of this, comparing Cupitt's call for a "new order" and his positive evaluation of Buddhism in *The World to Come* with Nietzsche's "madman" of *The Gay Science* and the condemnation of Christianity in *The Twilight of the Idols* and *The Antichrist*.[9] But surprisingly he misses Nietzsche's key phrase, "the revaluation of values," which for Cupitt is of great import:

> I started a really thorough reading of Nietzsche, and he made a huge impression on me in 1981. Since then I have been trying to do more on Nietzsche's thought and philosophy — to do that kind of drastic revaluation of everything. Our existing religions got their initial impulse two thousand years ago and they now are running out of steam. We do not just need a reformation — we need new religious thought.[10]

The Nietzsche project is underway, and although Cowdell discusses the consequences that this has for Cupitt's future writings, he fails to mention that "non-realism" has begun to take shape.[11] Cupitt first uses the term in referring to the religious outlook of the philosopher/theologian D. Z. Phillips:

> Alone among modern writers, he actually makes one think that an account of Christianity which is not based on belief that there is a metaphysical God out there might be religiously superior to the usual account.[12]

Phillips himself refuses to be categorized as either non-realist or realist, preferring to adopt an extreme Wittgensteinian stance concerning the separation of the language discourses of theology and philosophy, arguing for a position *against* both theological non-realism and theological realism. Phillips' concern is to clarify the grammar that both the realist and the non-realist use, i.e. to understand "the place concepts and beliefs have in human life".[13] Cupitt, while endorsing much of Wittgenstein, claims that his non-realism leads to quietism. He argues that Wittgenstein's emphasis on understanding what people are saying about God does not reckon with the fact that for religious realists "God" is more than a word in a language game. He later suggests that even if people admit that "God" is only a sign, worship can still function — just as economic exchange can continue when money no longer has the backing of a "real" gold standard.[14]

Cupitt pushes non-realism to its limit; the transcendent divine mystery becomes "the Ineffable." Thus he challenges his readers that "if (they) fully recognize the culturally evolved and symbolic character of religious beliefs, and see that beyond all the imagery and beyond the limits of language there is only and *can* only be the deep peace and silence of the Ineffable, (they) are liberated."[15] This again puts Cupitt in the mystical tradition, though the Kantian agnosticism and onto-theology is looking decidedly precarious. The Ineffable is deliberately obscurantist, leaving the reader to wonder whether there might be some grounding to the Universe after all. But, for Cupitt, that does not matter. The thrust of *The World to Come* is that such thoughts need not distract one. The Christian must journey to high ground, there to dwell with those Nietzscheans in the mountains of Hyperborea and to accompany St. John of the Cross to emptiness, the void, nihilism and non-realism. From this vantage point "the external world is an endless flux of phenomena, where we fully recognize that we can have no other point of view than our own, where we see that even the best knowledge available to us is still only provisional and of a status that is in principle uncertain."[16] The theist/atheist distinction cannot be stated in language; and in the end it does not matter for Cupitt. What is of prime importance for him is that religious beliefs are *expressive* of "a body of ideals and practices that have the power to give ultimate worth to human life."[17] This, not belief in a metaphysical God, has the power to save.

It can be seen, then, that Cupitt's "coming out" was a *gradual* and even painful process as he peeled off the layers of metaphysical realism and finally found "Nothing" at its core. In the next two books Cupitt "came out" with a vengeance, setting aside the deliberately obscurantist language and advocating a full-blown non-realism. *The Sea of Faith* and *Only Human* were written as apologetics for the non-realist cause.

The Sea of Faith (1984)
Only Human (1985)

The Sea of Faith was originally a series of six programs on BBC television. Cupitt was no stranger to television, having earned in 1977 the disparaging nickname of "TeleDon" from academics at Oxford and Cambridge Universities for writing a TV documentary with Peter Armstrong entitled *Who was Jesus?* Though today academics regularly air their views on the television, in the 1970s and 80s this was somewhat frowned upon. At that time to popularize (and by implication oversimplify) ideas that should be tackled only in university settings was an unpardonable sin. Cupitt quite correctly viewed *The Sea of Faith* as an opportunity to preach his non-realist gospel and to show that non-realism was a legitimate standpoint within Christianity, and one that had been held by many throughout the history of ideas. It was also an indication of the high esteem in which Cupitt was held by the media that the BBC should assume the risky undertaking of producing six "one-hour" television programs on a non-realist understanding of the Christian faith.

The Sea of Faith organized this project by pitting Christian non-realists against Christian realists (for example, Pascal versus Descartes). Much of the criticism levelled at Cupitt was precisely over his non-realist interpretation of many of his chosen portraits. The cudgel was especially taken up by Brian Hebblethwaite who replied with a book entitled *The Ocean of Truth*. Hebblethwaite moved from his earlier custom of "mildly denouncing (Cupitt) from the pulpit" to this full-blown attack:

> We can only conclude that Cupitt's prior commitment to an
> anti-metaphysical, expressivist, interiorised and pragmatic under-

standing of religious faith has dictated his choice of . . . figures
on the margins of modern Christianity who can, with varying
degrees of implausibility, be interpreted as pointing in this direction.[18]

David Edwards also accused Cupitt of "over-simplification" and "mis-
representation of Christians" such as Pascal, Schleiermacher and
Kierkegaard in order to fit them into his schematic summaries. He opined
that this misinterpretation of the historical facts has resulted in Cupitt's
"forfeit(ing) the admiration of many fellow academics by being a popu-
lariser wide open to expert criticism."

Obviously, Cupitt did not read his portraits in this way. He gave the
standard "postmodern" retort: "any text is capable of various readings, and
there is no such thing as the one True reading." When revising *The Sea of
Faith* for a reissue ten years later he reiterated his central thesis, arguing
that

we are always inside a language and a culture that shapes our
view of the world . . . we might view a religious belief-system,
not as a summary description of objective realities, but as a guiding vision and a programme for building a communal world.[19]

Moreover, he added, the old realism was now being taken over by a
larger movement of anti-realism (which included ethics and most of the sciences) that made non-realism *the* most satisfactory religious interpretation.

The TV series had an enormous impact. Cupitt received sixty or so
letters a day ("to that most unnatural of animals, an academic clergyman,"
as he was described by one of his correspondents) with many in agreement that non-realism is an acceptable position within Christianity.
However, while the feedback from the general public was generally favor-
able, many Church leaders were opposed to the position that Cupitt had
taken. Even the celebrated British anti-pornography and Christian moral
crusader Mary Whitehouse criticised the series — not for any salacious
content, but because of its radical Christian bias — and asked for a (conservative Christian)"right of reply of equal stature."

Cupitt voiced fears that there might be a heresy hunt against him.
However, while it is true that he never again was granted academic promotion and that others who advocated his non-realism were treated
severely, it is also fair to note that he was never hounded out of the ranks
of the clergy. Indeed, the only response of Robert Runcie to *The Sea of
Faith* programmes was a rather dismissive quip: "Cupitt is much cleverer
than I am, but I'm the Archbishop of Canterbury."

Cupitt was convinced that theologians must accommodate the insights of postmodernist writers. Thus, in *Only Human* Cupitt surveyed the non-realism inherent in the human and social sciences. Derrida replaces Kierkegaard and the book is in the style of Foucault through a kind of critical reflection on the history of ideas. Cowdell observes that *Only Human* is not "theological anthropology," since postmodernity is unable to insist on the primacy of the Christian story of fallen human nature.[20] However, he neglects to allude to some key concepts that will become crucial for Cupitt, who in an important passage takes his non-realism to its logical conclusion. The death of an objective God and the end of realism result in people focusing on

> The human world, which is the world of language, is alone: I call this new situation "anthropomonism." Try its implications for the question of death: it means that our life is what it is, it is bounded, it is all there is for us, and outside it there is nothing at all, not even nothingness. So, come back to the human world. You can no more step out of it than you can step out of the Universe of the modern cosmologists. Be content with what is.[21]

Cupitt's key themes of "anthropomonism" and "outsidelessness" centre him in postmodernism. Anthropomonism, as he explains thirteen years later, is a variant of the 'christomonism' used to describe Karl Barth's theology. Everett Tarbox Jr. correctly describes this stance as "the loss of the Archimedean point."[22] There is no reference point outside the human realm. The human world is all that there is and it is inextricably enmeshed in language. Thus, "the sum of all meanings and truths, all realities and values . . . is produced within and by the common conversation of humanity."[23]

Cupitt applies the Derridean shibboleth "there is nothing outside the text" to theology; the human world is "outsideless" — there is literally nothing "out there" — and the theologian must attempt to analyze this new state of affairs. Without recourse to another really existing world, one must try to comment on the meanings that have evolved in *this* world as a result of the interactions of human beings. Non-realism has naturally led Cupitt to embrace postmodernism. It is time to adopt Wittgenstein and kick away the ladder of realism that one has climbed for so long. It is time to address the issues raised by the end of modernity and end of realism. Two paradigm shifts of monumental importance have occurred: modernity has been replaced by postmodernity, and realism has been dissolved by anti-realism. What can religion and theology make of these shifts in thinking?

Stage 3

Postmodernism & Anti-realism
1986–1989

Cupitt's radical agenda is driven by his continual exigency to "keep up to date" with the latest philosophical and theological thinking. As early as *Christ and the Hiddenness of God*, he mentions that he has been disposed to reading theologians who might lead one to paths other than orthodoxy. In a conversation with his Cambridge supervisor George Woods, he reveals his "surreptitious" exploration into the thought of Kierkegaard. If one adds to this "a family trait: an extreme love of freedom" one ends up with a writer who "can't help being provocative," who is ready to embrace the "latest thing in religious thought," and hopes that he might see the day when others eagerly do the same.[1]

Cupitt plunges headlong into the latest postmodernist thought, attempting to reimagine Christianity and reinvent faith in response to the "four corners" of the postmodern world:

1. The self is constructed out of many cultural sources — the so-called "death of the self."
2. Moral and ethical discourses are forged out of dialogue and choice — everyone is an "ironist" or "constructivist" who recognizes that judgments are made "on the shifting ground of our own socially-constructed cultural worldviews."
3. No one style in art or culture prevails — people improvise and combine traditions to create their own lifestyles.
4. A global civilization is emerging — people freely cross cultural borders, erasing and re-constructing them.[2]

His next books engage these themes. In *Life Lines* and *The Long-Legged Fly* he intertwines theology with (1) and (3); *The New Christian Ethics* gives an answer to (2); and *Radicals and the Future of the Church* explores the kind of postmodern Christianity that will result. It is remarkable that (4) is not dealt with until 1997 when, in *After God*, he brings out the implications of what a global religion might be in a vision of "post-Christianity."

However, in the 1980s, Cupitt is concerned principally with Christianity (though in dialogue with Buddhism) and how it should interact with the postmodern world. He borrows religious symbols and themes from various sources and reinterprets them in light of the latest postmodern ideas. Thus, the notion of an endless flux of conflicting interpretations applies just as much to Christianity as to any other area of discourse. Christianity as it has been traditionally interpreted is collapsing, and Cupitt is in a revolutionary mood — promoting new religious thought and seizing ideas from hitherto unimaginable sources, most notably Continental and French postmodernist writers. Indeed for Cupitt, the strength of Continental philosophers, from Kant and Hegel to Derrida and Levinas, and even more recently Vattimo, has been their strong interest in theology.[3] While hardly orthodox in religion, the Continental philosophers recognize its importance as a serious human concern — something British philosophers have often failed to do.

Thiselton produces an excellent summary of Cupitt's use of French postmodernists, finding that in *The Long-Legged Fly* Cupitt's internalized God of non-realism vanishes with the death of the self.[4] This resultant loss, he argues, strips theology of its criteria and people become creators of their own meaning. To him this is simply a re-echoing of the Biblical story of Babel (Genesis 11), with confusion and chaos the hallmarks of a godless age.

Life Lines (1986)

Cupitt is not troubled by these accusations. His reading of Derrida dispels the Babel chaos of Thiselton, for he notes that postmodern deconstruction aims to demonstrate **not** the unlimited intentionality of a text, but the provisionality of "logocentric" truth and its own validity as "a form of critical reading." This interpretation of Derrida is actually endorsed by Derrida himself in the famous interview by Richard Kearney in *Dialogues with Contemporary Continental Thinkers: The Phenomenological Heritage*. Indeed, Cupitt is one of the few philosophers to have read Derrida correctly at this time. Hence it is totally inappropriate and injudicious of both Stephen White and Daphne Hampson to use Kearney's interview *against* Cupitt and to claim that Cupitt "misrepresents deconstruction."[5]

Cupitt reworks the story of chaos in Babel in *Life Lines* by what he terms "a Metro Map of the Spirit." The confusion that results when the Ultimates have been dispersed or de-centred does not lead to anarchy, but to a map on which you can locate your religious life route. The metro map is certainly a summary of Cupitt's own journey, leading from naïve realism through a crisis of belief in an objective God (station 9), via militant religious humanism (station 12), to the final station "Good Night" which combines Christianity with Buddhism. While Cowdell suggests that perhaps Cupitt wants his readers to stop at station 16 ("Good Night"), it is contrary to Cupitt's adopted postmodern outlook that one station can be thus privileged. Indeed, he states that "relativism is true relativistically" and so allows a place even for dogmatism.

Life Lines echoes postmodernism's emphasis on plurality, the end of foundationalism and an endless flux of conflicting interpretations:

> we have said that it is only because there is no truth, and instead merely a plurality of truths, that we have been able to rehabilitate the spiritual life, as being a pilgrimage through a long series of truths . . . this pilgrimage has no great destination and is never complete, but merely passes out into scattering and endlessness.[6]

This is exemplified in Cupitt's adoption of a *kenotic* reading of Christ who is dispersed in the communion meal, and of Buddhism where the self is dissolved and everything flows into its opposite. One must be ready to endorse many different stations of faith. The effect of postmodernism is to make Christianity protean. Like an amoeba it will change as people change, and one should not be afraid of the change but rather exult in being part of the flux.

The Long-Legged Fly (1987)

For Cupitt, postmodernism begins theologically with the death of God and philosophically with the end of foundationalism. Following these two losses, theology and philosophy must make a fresh start. Language is the new starting point because it is perceived to provide the most solid underpinning; and in *The Long-Legged Fly* "language" first begins to emerge as the "foundation" for his theological and philosophical "system".

The Long-Legged Fly is one of Cupitt's more difficult books for the general reader to tackle. It stretches the theological boundaries, forcing one to come to grips with Derrida's radicalizing of Heidegger and fathom the works of Continental thinkers like Jacques Lacan, Michel Foucault, Roland Barthes and Gilles Deleuze. Cupitt concedes that "the jargon is threatening," but insists that the key idea is quite simple. Since Cupitt's audience consists primarily of those outside academia, he tries to unpack complex arguments for everyday consumption. He explains the new post-modern thinking that has emerged in the last few years:

> The typically postmodern vision of the world is one in which there is no longer any absolute Beginning, Ground, Presence or End in the traditional metaphysical sense. So there is no anchor-age whatever, in any direction. To invert the spatial metaphor, the Centre is gone. There is only an immanent process of dialec-tical development without any inbuilt and overriding purposive-ness, and only a flux of differentiations without any substances or sheerly-given atomic units to build with. All explanation has now to be immanent and on one level, as in the dictionary every word's meaning is given solely in terms of its difference from its neighbours. . . . All explanation has to be sideways, and never up or down: such is our new form of naturalism.[7]

In order to translate these ideas into a metaphor that people can eas-ily understand, Cupitt appropriates the image of an insect — the pond skater (American "water strider") — that lives on the surface of many ponds. Like the pond skater, theology has to be horizontal; it can no longer exploit the familiar depths or claim transcendence. White accuses Cupitt of presenting a flawed idea, arguing that the same data could be used against Cupitt: the pond skater's apparently two-dimensional world, he argues, is actually created by the heights above and the depths beneath. It is from these other "realms" that both food and danger come, although the pond skater may never actually realise this until its two-dimensional world is invaded either from above or below. Thus for White "the pond skater's world is potentially more theistic than Cupitt perceives."[8]

The obvious retort is that White might himself be reverting to a flawed metaphor and reinstating the Old Testament three-decker Universe (the heavens above, the world on earth and the depths beneath).What is more, it must be remembered that Cupitt offers no more than an illustrative analogy, one which like all metaphors (including White's cosmology) breaks down when pushed beyond its limits. The metaphor of the pond skater sending out vibrations across the water as a means of communication is just that — a metaphor of the postmodern world as a communications network, a dance of signs, a naturalistic imma-nentism in which realism has been replaced by the ontological primacy of language. Cupitt's procedure is Cartesian: he doubts everything until he comes to that which cannot be doubted — language. His "language constructs reality" thesis now begins, and for the next decade this is the starting point of each new book.

However, we should not forget Cupitt's radical agenda, according to which nothing (not even language) is to be guaranteed ontological primacy forever. In 1998 *The Revelation of Being* will require language to cede an equal share of the stage to "Man" and "Being." To be sure, this anticipates yet another shift in Cupitt's thinking, but it also reveals the inherent danger of trying to force "closure" upon his ideas and of forgetting to ask, "Of which Cupitt are you speaking?"

The argument of *The Long-Legged Fly* is concerned with negotiating a religious path between the twin conflicts of legalism (culture) and lawlessness (desire). Using Lacan as an example of cultural stricture and Deleuze of extreme antinomianism, Cupitt dismisses both approaches on the grounds that the former is too heavy-handed and the latter too idealistic. Postmodernism calls for democratic societies in which new forms of life are tested and explored. This has led to the usual outcry from Cupitt's opponents: "What criteria can one use to test for these new forms of life?" Yet Cupitt is unconcerned by the calls for criteria. *That* betrays a realist way of thinking. There is no ultimate judge of meaning; there is no external fulcrum; and truths are comparable to works of art in that they have to be created by imagination and hard work.

Cupitt allies himself to the strictly anti-realist philosophical position that has infiltrated science (notably with Paul Feyerabend and Thomas Kuhn's "instrumentalism" and the "participant universe"), the Arts (e. g. the painting of Mondrian or the music of John Cage), and is now in theology as an extension of Nietzsche and the "death of God" movement (e.g. Thomas Altizer and Mark C. Taylor). John Bowker neatly expresses the anti-realist philosophical takeover:

> In . . . different domains . . . we can trace the collapse of realist ambitions with their displacement by a recognition of the relativity, incompleteness and subjectivity of virtually all our judgments. It is not just in Einsteinian relativity . . . nor simply in the shift to a participant universe: we can see it also in other major revolutions, in the recognition of cultural relativity in anthropology, in Gödel's theorem in mathematics, in conventionalism in the sociology of knowledge, in deconstructionism in literary criticism, in moral relativity and situation ethics in life, in the shift from tonality to atonality in music, in the move from

form to abstraction in sculpture, in the advent of the absurd in the theatre, in the "death of God" in theology.[9]

Perhaps the key to understanding Cupitt's theology in *The Long-Legged Fly* is his powerful use of the incarnation of Christ as a symbol representing our ability to overcome both the constraints of culture and our propensity for the unrestrained pursuit of pleasure. Cupitt is, contrary to popular opinion, **not** advocating "If it feels good, do it." A much more serious thinker than that, he is trying to steer a middle course between authoritarianism and excess. Cowdell gives an excellent summary of how postmodernism and incarnation are combined to present this "middle way:"

> In *The Long-Legged Fly* (1987) incarnation has come to symbolize the reduction of all meaning to purely human dimensions. There it is shorn of any sure ground, of any referent external to the diversity of human strivings. In part this is a statement of what rebel French philosophers such as Jacques Lacan and recent feminists are telling us — that culture imposes its values on us, that it writes on our bodies in fact, by language. But this is not at all a *fait accompli* for Cupitt. Christianity is also described as particularly . . . good at remedying the enslavement of desire to culture which he deplores — the reduction of people to unthinking passivity or uncritical obedience. . . . Incarnation thus becomes a metaphor for the nature of meaning in the post-modern world.[10]

This "middle way" is what makes Cowdell describe Cupitt as an "Anglican Apologist." And yet Cupitt remains as always dissatisfied with his (in)conclusion — seemingly uncertain about full-blown postmodern aestheticisation and also rejecting a return to modernism and realism. Cupitt reminds his readers that since *Taking Leave of God* the vertical axis of meaning has been lost and all that is left is the horizontal reading of the text from sign to sign. This he calls "linguistic naturalism." Language and the horizontal religious life are now aimed at ethics and the "future church," which become the themes of his next two books.

The New Christian Ethics (1988)

Although he published his study before the release of *The New Christian Ethics* Cowdell examined both this and *Radicals and the Future of the Church* in a paper presented at a seminar in New Zealand in 1991.[11] Despite being sympathetic to Cupitt, he differs from him in two ways.

First, he wishes to maintain theism (in a critical form) and offers post-modern alternatives to Cupitt by adopting a panentheistic redefinition of God. Cowdell tries to forge a path between the all-powerful, all-knowing God of theism and the rejection of God in atheism. He affirms a God who is beyond this world, yet also part of it. He combines transcendence with immanence in a "God for this world" who is nevertheless not defined by it (which would be to fall into the error of pantheism). The Christian God is in the world, yet not constrained by it. This is not the monster God of traditional theism which Cupitt abhors (and so does Cowdell), but the panentheistic God (advocated by liberal theologians such as David Tracy, Jürgen Moltmann, John Macquarrie and Process theologians) who "relates and suffers," and will survive "modern philosophical atheism and its problem of evil."[12] This is a constant theme of Cowdell and culminates in his book *A God for this World*.

Second, he admits that he cannot accept "a post-modern view of all reality as constructed within language alone."[13] Cowdell lists Foucault and Nietzsche as influences on Cupitt's debunking of the Christian salvation myth in favour of a perpetual espousal of humanistic causes that create new value in the world. For Cowdell, this radical Christian activism is essentially flawed because it has no theistic referent. Cupitt, however, sees no place for theism in the postmodern world. His major concern, since "coming out" is with the outcome of what it means to get rid of an objective God. Stephen Williams explains it thus:

> His difficulty ex professo was not the nature but the objec-
> tivity of God. A purported God of love that purportedly gives us
> freedom is still objective. . . . The impossibility of God is deduced
> from the facts of freedom and spirituality. He (*sic*) does not
> become the more possible by becoming the more benign.[14]

The New Christian Ethics is an attempt to answer the question about the *possibility* of Christian ethics in the light of the death of an objective God (non-realism) and the linguistic naturalism of postmodernism. In a nutshell, *how* can we create value in such a situation? The central argument of the book is that we should enrich and revalue the world by redescribing and cherishing our corner of it. This theme will be explored in depth in volume 2, but it should be noted here that this theme is a forerunner of Cupitt's later idea of "brightness" (2001). Language is steeped in evaluations, and we have to "make the world bright" (attractive) by the way that we use language. Language is more than the simple labelling of things; indeed, as the later Wittgenstein argued, language shapes our perception of the world. Words don't correspond to reality;

rather they create what we see, a process that involves an evaluation of the object of perception: "I like it" or "I don't like it!"

Central to this theme are Nietzsche's proposal of the revaluation of values and the proposition that Christian ethics is simply ethics produced by Christians. Values are constructed within a community. This creates a link to the social ethics of *The World to Come* and opposes the individualism of *Taking Leave of God*. Moreover, like all socially constructed ethical stances these values are provisional, and as such require continual examination and critique. Cupitt is not advocating utopianism (dismissed in *The Long-Legged Fly*), but piecemeal ethical conversation that criticizes and reforms the ethics already incorporated into society. The postmodern "constructivist" view of humans as "transient intersections in the human communications network" is ascendant, for only by interaction through and in language is public value created. The question that one is left to ponder is whether Cupitt's constructivism will make the world a better place? This question will be specifically addressed in volume 2.

Radicals and the Future of the Church (1989)

Cupitt's commitment to re-envisioning the churches, and in particular the Anglican Church, gains its fullest expression in *Radicals and the Future of the Church*. Dedicated to (the Reverend) Ronald Pearse — an Anglican clergyman who embraced non-realism — its aim is to assess the degree to which "in a postmodern age a *church* is possible."

Pearse's "coming out" was in the form of an article: "How Myth Could Enrich the Spirit," published in *The Times* newspaper in 1985. One of those who had been deeply moved by *The Sea of Faith* programs, he was especially convinced by Cupitt's call for an austere spirituality based on defending two "negatives" — (i) the non-existence of a metaphysical God and (ii) no belief in eternal life. Pearse equated these two "negatives" with "basic Christianity," arguing that the Christian liturgy should consistently reflect this sober spirituality. Yet he also wished to "balance" this austerity with an acknowledgment that Jesus displayed "an awareness of the richness of human relationships…the significance of everyday things and the importance of telling stories" — i.e. the necessity of myth. Pearse thus advocated a combination of spiritual austerity (the two negatives) and human myths (from the Bible, the church, and elsewhere) about "the fullness of life." This is what Christianity ought to be promoting. Amazingly, the reaction to Pearse's "coming out" was extremely muted. No follow-up articles or letters appeared in subsequent issues of the newspaper, and Pearse continued with no episcopal censure as Rector of the Anglican parish of Thurcaston. Perhaps the innocuous title of the article and the emphasis on myth helped deflect serious criticism — or even a perceptive reading of it.

In *Radicals and the Future of the Church* Cupitt takes up the attack levelled by *The Long-Legged Fly* against Lacan's (and Freud's) analysis of the imposition of cultural authority. Instead of hierarchy, he argues, the postmodern world promotes a "living horizontal network, a multicellular ferment of communication." People have begun to question and even dismiss the old hierarchies of domination. From the Green movement to liberation theology to feminism, the assault on realism — and in particular upon patriarchal discourse — has begun. In a world that decries domination, has no need for timeless norms and is fully post-historical, Cupitt attempts to describe what the church and human relationships might be like.

As an ordained representative of the kind of hierarchal organization that he so much despises, he finds himself in the doubly ironic position of creating new protocols of organization and belief for the Church. His academic position in Cambridge University bestows upon him the comfort and safety of a stipend, yet the incongruity of his ordained status and his radical agenda provides the opportunity for an opponent like Brian Hebblethwaite to call for his resignation:

> The Christian Church commissions its ministers to testify to the objective reality of God and to transmit the Gospel of the Incarnation. The Church is bound therefore to require of its ministers sincere faith in God. It would be absurd for Bishops to ordain atheists. And if an ordained minister loses his faith in God, it would seem appropriate for him, indeed incumbent upon him, to resign his orders.[15]

For Hebblethwaite, denial of an objective God is atheism and atheists cannot be ministers of religion. Cupitt defends his decision not to resign his ecclesiastical orders by saying that the only way to reform the church is from within, and that "Anglican formularies nowhere say either that the Church is infallible or irreformable, or that priests have got to be metaphysical realists."[16] Fully mindful that radicals within the churches might become easy targets for both liberals and conservatives, he prescribes for their survival in such an acrimonious atmosphere the strategies of evasion, deception and organised dissent.

Radicals and the Future of the Church contains much discussion about the necessity for the Church. Cupitt is still a churchman and remains within the Christian community, because of his double need for it. First, he argues that in an age threatened by nuclear obliteration as well as totalitarianism and terrified by the prospect of a tyrannical future, the Church can be viewed as offering an alternative value scale to that of the State. One thinks of the German theologian Bultmann who started going to church again as a protest against the Nazi tyrant Adolf Hitler. The Church was what you joined to indicate that you would not put your body and soul into the Nazi project. Similarly in the 1980s, with America and the Soviet Union at loggerheads, Cupitt accepted the argument that the Church provides a necessary alternative value scale, world-view, and defense of political and spiritual freedom in a world threatened by totalitarianism.

Second, Cupitt admitted in *The New Christian Ethics* that for years he had followed the Kierkegaardian path and was a Western religious individualist. Later, in 1994, he commented that Kierkegaard's extreme religious individualism and his conception of faith were both wrong and destructive, as evidenced by their effect on him personally and the angst-ridden nature of his last writings.[17] Although *Radicals and the Future of the Church* contains some talk of wandering the "hills" and self-imposed exile from the churches, Cupitt is adamant that he needs the church community. The aimless, joyful, wandering Bohemianism exemplified by the American theologian Mark C. Taylor's "Mazing Grace" is not part of Cupitt's radical agenda. He is wary of breaking away to set up a new denomination. Indeed he is adamant that radical Christians should stay and fight for their turf, plotting and scheming so that the conservatives do not win the day. Moreover, he sets out draft proposals of what a reformed church of the future will do and how it will be organised. It even seems as if his words of *The Long-Legged Fly* are to be fulfilled:

> Altizer writes that "Mark C. Taylor is the first American post-ecclesiastical systematic or philosophical theologian, the first theologian free of the scars or perhaps even the memory of Church theology" . . . but I fear that I for one am fated to be one of the last ecclesiastical theologians rather than one of the first post-ecclesiastical theologians. Which means that I have to be content to be "dotty."[18]

This "dotty" position that Cupitt finds himself in, becomes an unresolved tension. Is his message addressed principally to those inside or outside the churches? As the years pass, and with the emergence of the Sea of Faith Networks, Cupitt shifts more to those outside the churches, yet he finds it highly distressing to abandon radicals who remain within. It is perhaps fair to say that he never fully lets go of his love affair with the Anglican Church. Even today he is a member of a local congregation and attends Holy Communion services weekly — though he is also ready to describe himself as a "semi-detached member, willing to let the Church go." But that is once again to anticipate Cupitt, who in 1989 is still hopeful of reforming the Church *from within*, as his book tries to prove.

Anthony Thiselton claims that in *Radicals and the Future of the Church* Cupitt begins to take up a stance which is more "aggressively propagandist."[19] He laments this approach, especially the attack on liberalism and, more significantly, Cupitt's use of "the forked or double-pronged rhetoric" of the strategies of deception and evasion to disguise one's stance of "playing the game" from those in authority within the Church. Thiselton labels Cupitt's re-envisioning simply a "power bid" that wants radicals to be allowed to be "at ease" within churches in order to promote non-realism. He castigates Cupitt's posturing as postmodern "manipulative rhetoric," as opposed to "rational argument" (a polemic thrust that ironically makes Thiselton himself guilty of being "aggressively propagandist"). It is interesting that both Thiselton and Edwards are openly hostile to Cupitt, but when he replies in kind they berate him for being aggressive. Once Cupitt has brought the realism versus non-realism debate into the very heart of the Church, the antagonism seems to increase. Thiselton's hostile reaction is symptomatic of the unwillingness of both evangelical and liberal wings of the (Anglican) Church to permit Cupitt's radicalism a toehold.

Radicals and the Future of the Church marks a defining moment for Cupitt. He advances his non-realist thesis of *The Sea of Faith* and touts non-realism as a legitimate position within the Christian Church. Now the ecclesiastical theologians and authorities see they are confronted with much more than the maunderings of an off-beat lecturer at Cambridge University. It is significant that the Sea of Faith Network has begun in the United Kingdom, for this enables Cupitt to be more confident in pressing his non-realist cause. To this end he deliberately accentuates the realist/non-realist dichotomy. The postmodern insistence of *Life Lines* on relativism changes in *Radicals and the Future of the Church* to non-realism being a sort of "privileged narrative." This ploy is aimed, as Cupitt later argues, at allowing people "to kick away the ladder" of realism and embrace the horizontality of faith and life.[20] Stephen Williams chastizes Cupitt by recounting Hermann Hesse's book *Narcissus and Goldmund* which exemplifies the polarity between essentialism and creativity. Hesse's Goldmund is both an artist and a non-realist, but he does nothing to help those who suffer or are dying. Narcissus, on the other hand, holds on to belief in God and lives the pious life of the virgin monk. Of course, Williams acknowledges, Cupitt would agree that the non-realist Goldmund should have supplemented his Bohemian lifestyle with good works; but by Cupitt's analysis, simply because Narcissus is a realist, "he is irredeemable." Therefore, "because this must be Cupitt's conclusion, his own position is . . . irredeemably wrong."[21]

These are harsh words, yet they fail to recognise, as Thiselton noted, how Cupitt is using rhetoric and polarized positions to find accommodation within increasingly hostile churches. On the titlepage of *Radicals and the Future of the Church* he quotes Psalm 11:3: "If the foundations are destroyed, what can the righteous do?"(NEB). How can re-envisioning occur without an assault on "the foundations?" Cupitt is earnestly attempting to get the churches to endorse "a religion of life in the sense of a spiritual discipline that enables us to accept and to say yes to our life as it is, baseless, brief, pointless and utterly contingent, and yet in its very nihility beautiful, ethically-demanding, solemn and final."[22]

These themes — nihilism, ethics, and a religion that embraces the transitoriness of *this* life — will be explored by Cupitt over the ensuing years and into the next stage of his radical agenda — expressionism. Up to 1989 his central concern has been to help those who find his non-realist thoughts palatable, yet who sit perplexed and confused in the pews of realist churches. Significantly, Cupitt believes ethics to be the Trojan horse that will subvert Christian doctrine and bring about the triumph of radical theology. This links *The New Christian Ethics* with the solar ethics/expressionism that will surface in 1995. Cowdell rather optimistically declares that "there is little hope of a heresy trial," but it is certain that Christians who assent to non-realism will always be branded as troublesome by the church authorities. Indeed, Cowdell's prophecy will soon be shattered by the cases of two Anglican priests who champion the non-realist cause. Torquil Paterson, a lecturer at an Anglican theological college in South Africa, expressed his admiration for Don Cupitt and was asked by the Bishops to resign his position. In the United Kingdom the Reverend Anthony Freeman suffered the penalty for disavowing Narcissus' realism when his Bishop dismissed him from his parish for publishing a non-realist interpretation of the Christian faith. There were stormy times on the horizon both for Cupitt himself, and for his fellow radicals in the Sea of Faith Network(s). Still, he forged ahead, advancing non-realism as an acceptable theological position for church people, and he planned to travel to the Antipodes to explore with like-minded sojourners what the faith of the future might be. But, as I will show in the next stage, this proved to be far from an easy assignment. As Cupitt himself recounts,

> From about 1986 on, the strain grew. I was having more accidents, three times breaking bones. Late in 1991 I became very seriously exhausted.[23]

Expressionism-religion without God

1990–1997

The seven years between 1990 and 1997 were for two reasons the most demanding for Cupitt. First, he continued with a heavy workload of writing and lecturing yet still had professional commitments at Cambridge University. In addition to being a university lecturer and Dean of Emmanuel College, he held three other college posts and still tried to write *at least* one book a year. Second, the hostility of his opponents increased dramatically as he ventured overseas. One incident from a lecture tour in Australia in 1991 captures the intensity of feelings resulting from the perceived threat of his non-realist view of God:

> An archbishop there took the opportunity to denounce me and my ideas at a big church gathering. Afterwards, one of his cathedral clergy asked him why he had done this. 'Well,' replied the prelate reasonably: 'Privately, I've got a lot of sympathy for his ideas. But you can't say so, can you?' meaning that the leaders of the community cannot risk disturbing the faith of the common people.[1]

Cupitt had entered the international fray, but unfortunately his antipodean foray was also affected by "voice problems," for on several occasions he was forced to shorten his lectures or have someone read his scripts for him. Thus, towards the end of 1991, he had become totally exhausted by a decade of intense intellectual restlessness, overwork and public debating. His health deteriorated to such an extent that he suffered cerebral haemorrhages necessitating brain surgery to clip off an aneurysm in 1992. The physical *cost* that Cupitt has incurred to have his radical voice heard cannot be overemphasised. Indeed, David Edwards, one of his main detractors, correctly notes that Cupitt "has suffered considerably and that even though the words are dogmatic the lines of thought and pain are etched upon his face." It may be worth noting that he has survived much longer than a number of those who have influenced his thinking: Nietzsche, for instance, died at 56, Kierkegaard at 42, and Wittgenstein at 62. What is surely remarkable is that eight books and one booklet, together with numerous articles, were written during a period when Cupitt was often *in extremis*. He has outlined the difficult task that he has had to face:

> So far, very few radicals have proved strong enough to battle on for more than a few years. Most have cracked up or given up. I decided that the best contribution I could make was simply to stick it out, and try to build up a body of work that would be large enough to demand attention and cause lasting irritation, like the pearl in the oyster.[2]

Despite ill-health and increasing antagonism from fellow academics who sidelined him because of his radical writings, Cupitt was indefatigable when he found that he was not alone in his views. Increasingly he began to write for a steadily growing global network of supporters who were eager to discuss his ideas on how to reinvent religious thought. His next stage (Stage 4) — "expressionism" — attempted to offer those who journey on "the Sea of Faith" a way to express a faith that acknowledged the "death of God." It is therefore surprising to note that as late as 1999 a reviewer of Cupitt's books seemed ignorant of the existence of the network of followers, and accordingly could offer the wonderfully ingenuous observation that "if he had lived the recognized life of a new religious leader, instead of that of a Cambridge academic, he might now have a politically noticeable following."[3]

Cupitt, who is used to thinking two or three years ahead, remarked as early as 1988 that Cowdell's analysis failed to include his interest in expressivism. Expressivism, emotivism and expressionism are interchangeable terms for Cupitt. They are different ways of articulating the importance of a religious life that both represents "a continuous flowing creative process [that is] humanly constructed" and still "retains its own special place and authority in our lives."[4] This is especially relevant in postmodernity where the metanarratives have lost credibility, where we have to rely on "shifting positions," and metaphysics is replaced by fiction.

In this Expressionist Stage Cupitt attempts to answer Thiselton's concern that due to a proliferation of competing ideas, none of which could provide guidance as to how people should act or behave, postmodernism could lead only to despair. Thiselton had quoted the sociologist John O'Neill *against* Cupitt declaring that postmodernism, with no vision of a "beyond," promotes "social poverty and religious betrayal":

> What is degenerate about much postmodern celebration is that it lacks any religious sense of space and time. . . . In practice, the footings of postmodernism are sunk in fast food, information desks . . . and indifferent elevators that marry time and money to the second. The postmodern celebrants of the irreal, of the screen and its simulcra, ought to be understood as religious maniacs, or as iconoclasts breaking the gods, and not at all as sophisticates of modern science and art.[5]

Ironically, Cupitt would agree with much of this assessment of postmodernism! He too struggles to create meaning in a seemingly meaningless world. In a universe filled with a cacophony of competing voices, his main preoccupation is to create seemingly "out of nothing." The difference between him and Thiselton is that for Cupitt there must be a hermeneutics of de-objectification. As ever, he relies on the religious life to provide a humanly created, regulative ideal. Deprived of the frame of an objective God and facing nihilism, the question that Cupitt seeks to answer is, "What can religion without God offer to people?" During the next few years Cupitt (unlike most theologians who can only back away from it) dares to look into the nihil, embrace it, and advance expressionist religion in a bid to overcome it. His first book of Stage 4 attempts to delineate how it is possible to create religious meaning with no one or nothing "outside" to tell humans how they should conduct their lives.

Creation out of Nothing (1990)

In one of the very few autobiographical insights he had recorded up till then, Cupitt mentions an incident in Shepherds Bush, London in 1984 when he had a vision of "outsidelessness" which "bowls him over":

> How could language possibly take us right outside our human world and our human point of view? There is no outside. We always find ourselves already inside a language that was in place before we came along. We don't make it, it makes us. We are inside it, not it inside us . . . I realized that an outsideless prison is not a prison. There is only this! This contingent flow of verbal signifiers in which I am caught up, and which is outsideless, must be Being-itself, absolute Reality.[6]

If language is "all there is," then within the context of postmodernism language must find a way to describe a religion that is "not binary, not hierarchizing, and that does not devalue the manifest in favour of something beyond that is bigger, better and invisible." He wonders where this new language is being used, and by whom?[7]

Cupitt finds parallels with his anti-realism in the work of the American neo-pragmatist and non-representationalist, Richard Rorty. In particular he singles out the book *Contingency, Irony and Solidarity* in which Rorty argues that the vision of radical utopia is best created by reference to novelists and film makers. Yet, as always, Cupitt is never a "good follower" of another philosopher and though hugely sympathetic to Rorty, he argues that "to survive, in our postmodern universe made only of contingencies, relativities and interpretations," he needs "more resources" than novels or films. These resources are found in parts of the Buddhist and Christian traditions. From Mahayanan Buddhism Cupitt appropriates a spirituality that accepts utter transience or Nothingness. In Christianity he focuses on two specific events from the life of Jesus. First, he interprets the Sermon on the Mount/ the Plain (Matthew 5–7/Luke 6:17–49) as an invitation to live life in the eternal now (*nu*) for there is no consolation to be found elsewhere. We must devote all our efforts to bringing into being the kingdom in the here and now, creating just and more loving communities. Second, he understands the death of Jesus as a supreme act of confronting nihilism, its pathos rendered the more harrowing by his reported cry of despair from the cross, "My God, my God, why have you forsaken me?" (Mark 15:34//Matthew 27:46):

> (Jesus) . . . saw the Nihil as he died . . . and his having gone into it then helps me to go into it now. We are all going to have to put our heads into the black sock, you, me, everybody. He had to; but his despair may give us hope, if we can but bring ourselves to share it. Dying with Christ in the practice of religion, we go into the Nihil with him. We experience it while we are still alive. We die before death, and are thereby liberated for eternal, non-egoistic life now. If I have already died to Death in this way, I can accept my own insubstantiality and that of everything else, and live free from anxiety. That is religion. It is the triad, life-death-eternal life. It is a daily practice of death-and-rebirth as the basis of a productive life. It is an anguished mortal joy in life.[8]

Cowdell correctly notes that Cupitt is "reiterating his call from *The World to Come* that our culture needs a 'discipline of the void' to help us live with all this irony and contingency."[9] A religious discipline enables people to confront the utter arbitrariness of what happens. Almost anticipating his *Everyday Speech* books (written some eight years later), Cupitt discusses the famous sermon that the radical Bishop John A. T. Robinson preached after learning that he had been diagnosed with pancreatic cancer. Robinson argued that God was to be found *in* the cancer and not as the source or cause of the cancer, as Christianity had traditionally expounded sickness.[10] Cupitt feigns surprise that a Bishop should admit Nietzschean nihilism, yet then goes on to declare that even the most fundamentalist Christian realists, when confronted by the tragic circumstances of life, do not posit God as the direct cause of their tribulation. The early questions posed by Cupitt's hospital visits as a young curate in Salford begin to resurface. Just as he had then found that the best one could do was to offer the afflicted person guidance in coping with this seemingly random violence of existence, so now mainline Christianity has moved to this position. It does not seek to explain *why* a tragedy has occurred, only to give succour to the needy. The traditional Christian "problem of evil" is now bypassed:

> In the generation around the age of twenty a certain proportion of young people get knocked out by spinal cancer, schizophrenia, travel accidents — and we no longer even so much raise the traditional why-question. My religious friends, priests and theologians, nowadays actually prefer to accept like everyone else the unmotivated and arbitrary malignancy of life. . . . We are all of us nihilists nowadays. . . . Even those who claim to be theological realists turn out in the event to regard their own faith as something that helps them to survive and surmount evil, rather than something that helps them to explain it. The problem of evil has come to an end because we no longer think we have a right to expect the way things go to be, by itself and apart from our efforts, a moral story. But I can still think of faith as binding me to do my bit to try to make the way things go into a moral story.[11]

Religion provides a disciplined and therapeutic framework, which gives assistance to the sufferer to overcome adversity. This is the discipline of the void.

Creation out of Nothing contains a hint of the double bind of religion — "you can't do much with it, and yet you can't do without it." For Cupitt, the religion of realism is what one can't do much with, yet a new

religion that brings to an end all dualisms and Platonic thought is the one
thing one can't do without. Like Lloyd Geering who, updating the French
"functionalism" of Emile Durkheim, argued that religion acted like "superglue" binding a society together and avoiding the pitfalls of individualism,
Cupitt sees the value of religion properly understood as a human creation
capable of overcoming nihilism:

> Religion is a here-and-now conquering of nihilism and a re-
> creation of our world out of nothing by continually generating
> new metaphors and new interpretations. . . . So religion is a kind
> of creative art by which we make ourselves and our world, end-
> lessly revaluing the familiar and minting new metaphors. All
> major cultures have their own characteristic set of religious
> metaphors and rituals, and in every culture the central religious
> concepts and symbols provide the vocabulary in which people
> articulate their sense of life's meaning and worth. Religion is only
> human, but no culture survives for long without it. Life's mean-
> ingfulness and worthwhileness are not given but have to be
> made, and that making is religion.[12]

Two themes now begin to emerge: the theologian as artist, and the
aestheticisation of religion. Cupitt discussed the paintings of the
American artist Mark Rothko in *Radicals and the Future of the Church*,
emphasising that art fulfils a religious function with the artist given status
as a living creator now that the Christian tradition is at an end. Cupitt
goes one step further by endorsing performance art — especially the work
of Richard Long, who travels afoot through many parts of the world select-
ing "earthy" materials that will become the subject matter of his work.
For Cupitt, Long's walking and his work are metaphors for the continuing
possibility of a dedicated and creative religious life. Just as his tramping
the hills and deserts leaves a trace on the earth, so our discipline of the
void will leave a sacred trace on the world. The sacred is not to be found
in the apprehension of a divine Being, but in a religious life that is thoroughly naturalistic, humanistic and *this* worldly. In an article in the cata-
logue of an art exhibition, *The Journey*, staged in the Usher Gallery in
Lincoln, Cupitt writes that "Long's chosen materials, rocks and mud,
stood at the bottom of the old Chain of Being" and "it was the intention
of the artist for us to stop at them" because the "Sacred stays on the land
surface, and we should stay there too."[13]

The implication is clear. Postmodern nihilism *can* be made hospitable
in the knowledge that *this* world is all that *we* have, and that new non-

dualistic and non-Platonic religious ways of living can be created "out of nothing."

What Is a Story? (1991)

The reaction to *What Is a Story?* has been extremely mixed. Some university departments of English have adopted it as a primary text. Others, following Thiselton, dismiss it as being "lightweight," arguing that Cupitt has not engaged seriously with the current literary theorists. Thiselton, like many of Cupitt's critics, takes up his position from "an immense height of assumed intellectual superiority."[14] He castigates Cupitt for his flawed "passing allusions" to Barthes and Lyotard, and failing to "engage with narrative theory at a serious level through such seminal thinkers as Gérard Genette, Paul Ricoeur and Seymour Chatman."[15] Thiselton has a special interest in Ricoeur, whose *Oneself as Another* provides the basis for his own thesis. Ricoeur undermined both the Enlightenment project of the autonomous self and the postmodern decentred self by arguing for a self in relation and rooted to a universal Being. Thiselton builds on this work; he argues that the self is not all surface or flotsam, but is in relation to the Divine "Other," which is the call that summons from beyond. This coheres with the self found in Scripture, a self always in relation to the God who "beckons from beyond to invite new hope, new promise, even resurrection."

Graham Ward correctly identifies the fault line that divides the realists and the idealists (anti-realists). He observes that the decisive difference that separates R. B. Braithwaite, Janet Soskice, and Sallie McFague (and I would add Thiselton, Cowdell and most critical realists) from Mark C. Taylor (and Cupitt) is that "the latter (two) deny and the former (group) assert a division between experience and language, truth and expression, reality and representation."[16] With this in mind, it should come as no surprise that Cupitt would not be on the same page as Paul Ricoeur! It seems not only illogical of Thiselton to complain that Cupitt eschews someone on the opposite side of the theological and literary fence, but clearly indicative of the polemical nature of his thesis.

What Is a Story? is an espousal of the idealist (anti-realist) position that stories produce reality, shaping our lives both individually and corporately. Following on his expressionist path, in the light of the postmetaphysical and postmodern situation which people now inhabit, Cupitt argues that religious narrative or stories provide earthly fictions to help people cope with life. Whereas the realist insists on a highest Truth that must be beyond narrative and timeless, Cupitt and anti-realists bring a multiplicity of truths down to earth. White astutely notes that Cupitt makes a minor shift from language to story. It is "story that becomes the prime medium of human communication" because it is through story that people "express" their deepest hopes and fears.[17] And in story they attempt to transcend the mundane happenings of their lives. This seems to put Cupitt in a paradoxical position — and almost back into the arms of Ricoeur. But Cupitt will not be so led. He accepts that hopes of transcendence are needed, yet insists that the myth of transcendence will incongruously return us to this world. It is when people cannot face up to the transience and contingency of their situation that they import the religious myth of the Beyond. Importantly, however,

> The task of religion is not to gratify this incoherent yearning, but to cure us of it by telling us stories. The moral of all Christian stories is: "Give up those illusory mystical yearnings, accept the human condition, love your neighbour, pour your own life out into the common life of all humanity. In a word, give up God and be content with Christ."[18]

Here Cupitt is already anticipating his *Everyday Speech* books that appear almost a decade later, for in them he argues on the one hand that the language of everyday speech affirms the value of life, yet on the other recognizes the effects of the encompassing threats to life. In 1991 Cupitt presents much that same position, but emphasizes story (especially religious story); a decade later everyday speech has itself become the religious story. Concluding the book, he is aware of having fallen foul of the postmodern paradox which Lyotard noticed. To proclaim the end of grand narratives is itself to reinstate another grand narrative, namely that by our stories we are "continually retelling, embroidering, making it up as we go along." And the point of all this is "the conviction that our life still matters, fragmentary and fictitious though it is."[19] Likewise, it is principally to the Christian story that Cupitt looks for this conviction. In particular, he echoes his Christological outlook in *The Long-Legged Fly* where Jesus, following Nietzsche, came to urge the revaluation of values:

> His promise of the Kingdom of God to the poor is precisely the sort of promise of revaluation to the devalued that we still need to hear. His fate is a reminder that the human scene will not become less cruel until we begin to dismantle the old machinery of victimization. His life-story can still encourage us

to take up the cause of something or other that is currently unpopular . . . and it still embodies the old values of love and reconciliation. Reimagined, those values can yet become ours, too.[20]

What Is a Story? is a pivotal book. Having reaffirmed the outsidelessness of existence and the postmodern condition stated so boldly in *Creation out of Nothing*, it then tries to *find a way out of it* through story. We yearn to be freed of "the nihil" (nothingness) and so create the myth of transcendence. However, it is only a myth and we must likewise take our leave of it. Once that is done, we are returned to the world to which we must dedicate ourselves. Cupitt's master-narrative is that religious expressionism is not afraid of the nihil and that life matters. The stories of religion, especially some of those in Buddhism and Christianity, express the theme that transience is eternal life and that one should say "Yes to Life," warts and all! All meaning and truth is linguistically made up, and only through our stories do we constitute the world and humanity as intelligible entities. In short, humanity invents and reinvents itself according to itself. The Christian grammar of incarnation is displaced by socio-linguistic grammar that permits redemption in the here and now by the dedication of our lives to causes that enhance the lives of others.

Cupitt has been threatening to bring out the full implications of his being repeatedly labelled by his detractors as "just a Buddhist." Turning this ostensibly abusive remark against his opponents, he says that it is "rather an honour for a Westerner to be thought to deserve that name."[21] However, apart from a few fleeting references and a section of a chapter in *What Is a Story?* on Zen Buddhism, Cupitt's radical agenda has so far been aimed squarely at reenvisioning Christianity. In *The Time Being* Cupitt first focuses his attention on Buddhism, and in particular the Japanese Zen Buddhist teacher, Dōgen.

The Time Being (1992)

The Time Being is an example of Cupitt's penchant for punning and allusive titles and catchwords. The title of the book refers not only to Japanese Zen Buddhist, Dōgen's treatise on *Uji* (Being-time), but also to Heidegger's "classic" *Being and Time* as well as W.H. Auden's *For the Time Being*. Dōgen, who has been described as the "Japanese Meister Eckhart," taught a mysticism of transience that resonates with the idea that postmodernity is a world of signs in which everything is "aestheticized and has turned into a flux of transient cultural products." Traditional Christianity has insisted that everything is fixed and immutable, but both Zen and the

Madhyamika variety of Mahayana Buddhism have been teaching the opposite for centuries. They represent a religion of utter contingency.[22]

Cupitt finds within Mahayana Buddhism a truly postmodern religion that includes non-realism and endorses eternal happiness — not in another world, but in saying "Yes" to this one. Cupitt advances what he labels: "a post-Buddhism of the sign" or the "mysticism of secondariness." By this he means that a deconstructed religiosity is today very widespread and has much influenced modern art ever since the Impressionists. He admits that something that started him off on this was his visit in the mid-1980s to the home of French Impressionist Claude Monet, in Giverny. Seeing Monet's lily ponds and Japanese bridge, and reflecting on his final paintings, Cupitt recognized that the late-impressionist vision of the world, with its attempt to break out of realism, was very close to a Buddhist vision — the mysticism of everything transient and fleeting. Monet's visual delight in immediate experience exemplified what religion should do — "go light, delight in life, delight in experience, delight in how the world pours out and passes away." The preponderance of light and shadows, water and flowers had long been familiar to those in China and Japan, but were new in the West; and Monet's Giverny home and many Japanese landscapes showed the affinity between Japanese Buddhism and Impressionism.

In the 1980s and 1990s, the Western world, under the influence of postmodernist thought, suddenly awakened to the realization that everything is endlessly transient and impermanent. The result was unease and discontent. But Eastern thought had for centuries offered a remedy that Cupitt advises us to consider: a spirituality of acceptance of temporality that can transform the Western tradition. As Dōgen's treatise simply states: "whatever happens or is, is not in time, but is time."[23]

Cupitt appropriates Buddhist thought to continue his search for a way of going beyond or coping with the postmodernist condition. How might one find a valid religious way of accepting insecurity and secondariness? The answer is that one must not become swallowed up by these concerns or escape them by the flight to realism, but adopt a religious approach to living that accepts them. For the first time, Cupitt frankly admits that we "*need* a religion without God," but then immediately qualifies this to mean "a religion without absolutes, without perfection, without closure, without eternity."[24] Reinterpreting the Japanese poet Matsuo Basho (1644–1694) against his translator Yuasa, Cupitt argues that Basho's poetry, especially in the *haiku* about a frog, is an expression of the acceptance of the fleetingness of everything and is an image of eternity. It is:

An art-unity of word and feeling in the passing moment, with which one is content. The frog hits the water, glop, and a little poem takes shape in Basho's mind. Does that give a hint how there might be a religion of transience, free from the illusion and time-hate we know too well?[25]

The role of "religion without God" is to be therapeutic in that it helps people cope with things the way they are. However, just as one begins to think that Cupitt is going to fully embrace Buddhist teachings, he detaches himself from them, declaring that they still deny both the truth of outsidelessness and the priority of language:

They hang on to some sort of ghost of the idea that there is a silent space somewhere outside time, language and the passions. While they cling to this residuum of the ascetical outlook, they are not yet saying a full religious Yes to time, the passions, language and death. And that's what we must do. . . . There can be no other Way to salvation except by saying Yes to time, language, the passions and death — in short, to just about everything that our religions hitherto have been in flight from.[26]

Then, thanking Buddhism for its insights, but not completely content with what he views as too much emphasis upon "an ethic for the retired," Cupitt turns again to radical Christian humanism. For him there must be an "active" as well as passive component to the spiritual life and, as he will elucidate in his next book, *After All*, there must be both expressive and contemplative religion. How accurate, then, are the claims that he is really a Buddhist in disguise? Gregory Spearritt has correctly noted that despite extensive areas of agreement and similarity between Cupitt's ideas and Buddhist thought — especially in the "lack of hierarchy," the emphasis on right action rather than right belief, and the lack of ideology — they diverge in two very important respects. First, Buddhism tends to be negative towards the conventional world and strives to escape it, whereas Cupitt "accepts and affirms the world despite viewing it as nihilistic." We cannot escape from it and it "should engage us wholeheartedly." Second, Buddhism recommends the transcending of dualities and distinctions whereas Cupitt views the world as "entirely language-formed and thus inevitably involving distinctions."[27] Consequently Cupitt might be described as a "semi-detached" Buddhist, taking what he wants from it and raiding other traditions for the rest of his religion without God.

In Chapter 8 of *The Time Being* Cupitt prepares the ground for his "active non-realism" — which in 1995 will be released as "solar ethics." Buddhism has proved too negative in its acceptance of the *status quo*. Despite what many of his critics allege, Cupitt's attitude towards our social conditions is **not** to declare: "C'est la vie!" Nor does he ask his followers to chant: "Che sarà sarà." Cupitt's radical agenda is not so quietistic. He argues that all of us, even enclosed order silent monks, are involved in the world (the "human theatrical show") by the various roles that we play. However, he admits that the extent to which people can challenge or change those "on top" of the social order is limited, arguing for recourse to "laughter, cunning, deviousness, or some other weapon" with which to make them uncomfortable.[28] This coheres with Cupitt's anti-utopian stance in *The Long-Legged Fly* and his emerging "transactional" ethics that equates truth with the current state of the argument, and sees change as coming about through conversational exchange, negotiation, and persuasion. This point will be discussed extensively in volume 2, where I will argue that it does not leave Cupitt open to charges that his decentred spirituality can work only in an openly democratic political system.

Cupitt concludes *The Time Being* by urging his readers to forget the book and "outdate" him. He offers two reasons. First, he thus reiterates the postmodern theme of the democratization of knowledge in the absence of a fixed authority and challenges the idea found in some religions that only a select few have "The Answer" for the masses. Second, he prepares the way for others to take up his mantle and promote non-realism because he does not expecting to be alive — or at least not active — for too much longer. This latter point can be seen especially in the final words of *The Time Being*. Cupitt originally wrote "Farewell" fearing that he might either fail to recover from scheduled neurosurgery at Addenbrooke's Hospital, Cambridge or be incapacitated by the poor mental health that was then troubling him. Upon correcting the proofs, however, he had second thoughts and split the word to read "Fare well." In the two-year interval before his next book, three members of the United Kingdom Sea of Faith Network responded to that call to "move on" — Hugh Dawes, David Hart and Anthony Freeman.[29] Even if Cupitt were to do so, the radical agenda would not be allowed to die.

After All (1994)

The cover photograph of *After All: Religion without Alienation* reveals that Cupitt has survived his neurological operation, although the gaunt visage shows that he is still far from in perfect health. The lack of any attempt at a make-over suggests that the point is the "joy in affliction" theme of the book. Indeed, Cupitt admits in 1998 that: "the real topic of the book was a few moments of happiness so great that for their sakes it was permissible to set out to make the entire book happy."

In *After All*, Cupitt continues with the modality of expressionism, and addresses himself to two major concerns. First, he proposes the emergence of post-Christianity. This he equates with the Kingdom theology that he claims was *the* original message of Jesus subsequently distorted by ecclesiastical Christianity. Ecclesiastical theology is a mediated and hierarchical system that subjects people to authority and discipline. Kingdom theology is immediate, non-hierarchical, and egalitarian. It doesn't care about distinguishing "us" from "them," "the sound" from "the unsound" for it just *is*, it calls itself into being and it is happy with life. The Kingdom is the Church's conscience. The Kingdom is what Jesus promised, the Church is what happened; and the Church is a poor substitute for the Kingdom. The Church constantly idolizes itself and represses the Kingdom. It doesn't want Christ to come and it doesn't want the Kingdom. It prefers the hierarchy, the mystery, the authority and power. Second, he uses much of the book to argue that the anti-realist vision is congruous with the latest scientific world view. Central to both these concerns are themes that we have encountered in the preceding years: "our world is the human world, a world bounded by language, time and story, and radically outsideless; there is only the flux of language-formed events and the flux is outsideless; this is 'all there is' and there's nothing wrong with all this; and the role of religion is not to take us out of this world but simply to reconcile us to it."[30]

Using many of the forerunners of "non-realism" that figured in *The Sea of Faith*, Cupitt sketches the historical antecedents of post-Christianity, especially between 1775 and 1845 (Immanuel Kant to David Strauss), contesting that Christianity has the capacity to demythologize itself and become something more than itself. Indeed, he traces this idea back to Jesus himself — the first post-Christian — whose message was that people could live without ideology, and who attacked "traditionalization, codification and objectification." This was the central theme of Jesus' Kingdom theology and hence the subtitle to Cupitt's book: "Religion without Alienation." It is a bold assertion which finds Cupitt relying for his Christological claims on the work of Geza Vermes' *The Religion of the Jesus the Jew*, together with a restatement of a major figure from *The Sea of Faith* — Albert Schweitzer. The latter he argues was a proponent of metaphysical agnosticism who believed in Jesus and his kingdom of ethical world affirmation, reverence for life, ethics of love and world peace. This interpretation of Schweitzer has been vigorously challenged. Brian Hebblethwaite, in particular, argues that Schweitzer himself did not respond to his unfavourable discoveries about the historical Jesus by forsaking a realist faith in God. Hebblethwaite argues that despite the inconsistency between Schweitzer's reconstruction of Jesus' motives (most notably in *The Quest of the Historical Jesus*) and his own understanding of an undeniable ethical calling of "reverence for life," he still believed in a transcendent deity.

The evidence is inconclusive as to whether in fact Schweitzer retained or abandoned belief in an objective God. The key texts are Schweitzer's doctoral dissertation on Kant's philosophy of religion, and a lecture on Nietzsche, which is unfortunately now lost. Cupitt himself agrees with those commentators on Schweitzer who say that he was not a realistic theist. There is enough evidence he holds, to put the point beyond doubt. Indeed, whatever the final verdict, the *implications* of Schweitzer's ethical stance that favor Cupitt's voluntarist post-Christianity still stand. Even such a conservative theologian as Karl Barth could see in Schweitzer's ethic of reverence for life "an outcry" — "an affirmation of the world and of life which was also at a deeper level a cry of protest and pain."[31] Accordingly, whether Schweitzer's belief or non-belief in God can ever be proved, his ethical imperative can still be used. Post-Christianity, together with its corollary Kingdom theology, will occupy Cupitt's radical agenda in the ensuing years. He will argue that Kingdom language has already entered everyday speech, and its themes of immediacy, non-hierarchy, the democratization of religion and politics, outsidelessness, and reverence for all life are what people now seek from Christianity; unfortunately, they receive the opposite teaching from the churches. This is to anticipate Cupitt, however, and involves issues that will be discussed later.

Cupitt's other concern in this book is the marrying of anti-realism with scientific thought. In a very long chapter entitled "How It Is" (nearly half the book), he argues for the need of a new "metaphysical doctrine": that there exists only "one (immensely tangled and dense) flow of events, but it is always overlaid and formed by language; that is, it is always *read* in one way or another."[32] Acknowledging the late writings of Georges Bataille, and using the metaphor of the fountain from George Berkeley, his anti-realist metaphysic enables one to rush headlong into the ambivalence that is life. Affirming Nietzsche's pronouncement that "the world is a work of art that continually gives birth to itself," the anti-realist defines and redefines who and what he/she is, in and through the stories or fictions that he/she invents.

No one is "sacred" for the anti-realist, and Cupitt takes a swipe at the scientific realism of one of the leading cosmologists of the day, Stephen Hawking. He calls into question Hawking's disparaging remarks about the primacy of language in *A Brief History of Time*. Cupitt's attack on the scientific establishment's tendency "to overlook their own linguisticality" recalls that of another "maverick" anti-realist — the philosopher of science Paul Feyerabend, whose most celebrated book is *Against Method: An Outline of an Anarchistic Theory of Knowledge*. This contains his famous remark that the epistemological anarchist "has no objection to regarding the fabric of the world as described by science and revealed by his senses as a chimera that... [is] a mere web of dreams that reveals, and conceals, nothing." Cupitt equates Feyerabend's "overcoming epistemology" in philosophy with his own project of "overcoming orthodoxy" in theology, that of simplifying things to: "We don't need a policeman." People must be free to generate their own theories of knowledge, their own stories about the natural world and their own ideas about God. For expressionists, "like us, God is made only of words."

To be sure, some of the emerging Sea of Faith Network writers are anti-realist in theology but philosophically realist: an example is Graham Shaw, who sides with Iris Murdoch in maintaining realism in ethics while denying the existence of a metaphysical God. Cupitt, however, is an extreme, thoroughgoing anti-realist. He adopts totally the concept of *everything* as a dance of signs that pours out and yet renews itself with no recourse to anything Beyond. Enlisting the aid of such diverse metaphors of a fountain, Siva's ring of fire, the circles of Dante's cosmology, and Nietzsche's myth of the eternal return, Cupitt drives home his anti-realist, "outsideless" vision where redemption entails fully immersing oneself in a cycle of dying and rebirth.

Thiselton criticizes Cupitt for this metaphysic, claiming it is hasty and ill- considered to dispense with the "mind/matter problem that has occupied the best philosophical minds for centuries." Cupitt, of course, would respond that since the human subject embodies no "inner mind/consciousness," one can hardly hypothesize a mind that plays an active role in shaping and forming our world. Instead, language itself, understood as the endless to and fro of human symbolic exchange, is the sole shaper of the world. The mind plays no "constructive" role in shaping our experience, because experience is pre-formed by language. The world is not situated "inside our eye-sockets or visual cortex" and given shape and form, but is played out in front of us — it is our field of view. Indeed, Cupitt defines thoughts as "unspoken words."

Cupitt's book ends with a "twin-forked" religion that can help one with "how it is" — i.e., the anti-realist vision of the world. Cupitt advocates both contemplative **and** active religion, yet he redefines their meanings. Traditionally, Christianity has considered that contemplation involves stillness and quietude and withdrawal from the world. By attending retreats and adopting contemplative techniques (normally associated with monasticism) Christians have attempted to throw off the cares and chaos of their lives and in solitude glimpse the Beyond. By freeing themselves of the burdens of this world, they have sought holiness, purity, and truth from another world, and a foretaste of the heavenly Kingdom that is to come. For Cupitt the opposite is now the case. If this world created by language "is all there is" then everything is "relative and fleeting." Hence he redefines contemplative religion as "ecstatic immanence" where the ambivalence that is a mark of all existence (being "alive," yet recognising that life is very transitory) can be overcome by loving and being absorbed in that transience. We must contemplate living in *this* world of transitions, rather than seek in vain for a meditative technique that will transport us from this world to the next. Contemplation is understood as "surfing the moment" and people are "energies read-as-signs" who find mean-ing (there are no fixed meanings) in "ecstatic immanence." They learn to love to jump back into immanence and not look outside, for there is no outside. Dedicating *After All* to his wife who is an accomplished potter, he invokes the image of her at her pottery wheel, totally engrossed in her craft, as an example of the contemplative religion he labels: "ardent creative self-expenditure."

In case one is left wondering whether Cupitt is simply advocating a return to some sort of contemplative mysticism, he then proposes that people actively try "to make the world *that* beautiful." Again Cupitt relies on transactional ethics as the way of achieving this, because the anti-realist vision has conceded that "we made it all up, for we finish it as we appropriate it through language." As language leads to more language, it must be acknowledged that words (and this includes ethics) have no meaning except that given by social and cultural norms. Cupitt has thus sided with Heraclitus, Darwin, Nietzsche and Bataille in acknowledging that conflicting and often violent forces have created the world. This is also the message of Jesus, especially in the Sermon on the Mount:

in his own Kingdom-religion, Jesus of Nazareth did not envisage a peaceful restored Eden. On the contrary, the Sermon on the Mount throughout envisages the continuation of stress and conflict, persecution and suffering. But he promises joy in affliction: no more, but no less than that.[33]

The anti-realist vision, Cupitt's metaphysical doctrine of language, and an understanding of Jesus' message of the Kingdom all coalesce to express a new "religion without alienation," a coherent and democratically constructed view of life for a fragmented postmodern world. Cupitt is gradually assigning features to his vision of a "religion without God."

The year 1995 brings with it two books that deal with the emerging twin poles of expressionism — Christian humanism as post-Christianity (*The Last Philosophy*), and ethics as spirituality or a way of living (*Solar Ethics*). As usual, Cupitt's first concern is his philosophical anti-realism, which is the *only* (last) philosophy.

The Last Philosophy (1995)

Originally entitled, *Felicific Philosophy*, and then, *Easy, Going, The Last Philosophy* is, on Cupitt's own admission, "a little apart from what I have written hitherto." Commencing as a series of lectures at Cambridge University, its thesis was also debated by the "D" society, the Cambridge University Graduate Philosophy of Religion Seminar group at which well-known philosophers/theologians presented papers. Cupitt inserts comments from both groups within the text. This, together with its twenty-two point headings (plus Appendix), makes it a sort of "work-in-progress" type of book, one that could be described as a summary of the many expressionist themes that have been encountered since 1990. Indeed, Cupitt hastily claims (there are in fact three more expressionist books to follow!) that "this essay may be read as completing the 'expressionist' series of books."

Cupitt's reason for writing *The Last Philosophy* is to give an account of the philosophy that underpins his philosophical theology. He also anticipates his next-but-one stage, a turn to ordinary language. Four years later in *The New Religion of Life in Everyday Speech* he will declare that not only have people in their ordinary language taken on board this "new" (anti-realist) way of thinking that is consistent with his radical agenda, but they have thus shown themselves "significantly sharper than the professionals." Cupitt enlists the services of one of his non-realist heroes of *The Sea of Faith* — Ludwig Wittgenstein. He admits that is he faced with the same difficulty as that which confronted Wittgenstein — attempting to centre religious and philosophical thinking in the here and now and in the world of ordinary language and ordinary life. Like Wittgenstein he does not wish to "take in any foreign goods" in the sense of being taken captive by other philosophers or their philosophies. Unlike Wittgenstein, who refused to read other philosophers, Cupitt is content to be irritated by them and even acknowledges a debt to many of them (see his "Prosopography" for a list of those who are "clues of a private mythology...and a key to the writer's personal canon").

Philosophy's Own Religion (2000) is largely a reprise of the themes of *The Last Philosophy* (1995), with Cupitt concerned to unpack the underlying significance of philosophical anti-realism. In 1995 it was very much **his own** philosophical system, but by 2000 he has recognized that the language of ordinary, everyday speech has been espousing anti-realism for many years! Thus, in the space of only five years he will move from being the academic who **tells** people what is the best philosophical system to embrace, to being one who simply **describes** what philosophical system is currently reflected in everyday speech. The function of philosophy and religions will no longer be prescriptive, but descriptive.

In 1995 Cupitt was still the academic who reinterprets the way things are for "ordinary folk," hoping to "to write a kind of philosophy that is genuinely accessible to the ordinary reader, while also being avant-garde, and holding nothing back." Graham Ward neatly condenses the central argument of the book:

> (We) rehearse once more the language-constructs-reality thesis, the commitment to a philosophy of life in which the nature/culture distinction is no longer determinative, and the call to a disseminated self to go with the flow and experience an immanent ecstasy. . . . We are compelled to read, compelled to sojourn though a holographic *Lebenswelt* in which aesthetic pleasure replaces meaning. . . . The philosophy itself propounds a cosmic humanism: the world as Anthropos. It is, and Don Cupitt states this, monistic.[34]

Ward considers that this "monist cosmic humanist" philosophy runs counter to the postmodern emphasis of Derrida, Lacan and Foucault (all of whom Cupitt calls upon) on différance, alterity and a plethora of interpretations. How can Cupitt now announce there is only "one" philosophical system? He further accuses Cupitt's philosophy of returning to "an Hegelian totalizing in need of deconstruction" and that a system of "going with the flow" does not adequately appreciate the "sheer violence that adheres to difference" because there are many flows, not one. Cupitt would wholeheartedly agree; indeed he has anticipated his opponent! He actually makes provision within the text for such an objection, clearly remarking that having stated his system he ought to put it under erasure lest people accuse him of relapsing "into an obsolete kind of metaphysics." For on his own premises our thinking is constrained "by the forms of representation available to it; that is, by our language."[35]

Still, it should be acknowledged that throughout this expressionist period Cupitt attempts to provide some sort of resolution (if only partial) to the ambivalence that haunts the self and the world. It is only by expressing ourselves through language that we create a common world — and then because of restlessness and dissatisfaction continually recreate it and make it more human(e). This is cosmic religious humanism. No utopian dreams or Augustinian City of God are to be found, but by our common artistic engagement in the work, the world is created and recreated. Cupitt's emphasis is on finding reconciliation with this world "as it is now." He "repent(s) of (his) former self-conscious strenuousness" and, as "death gets closer (he) becomes easy, going" — appealing to an ethic of world-love and being "at home" in the Universe. When you become "easy, going" you are unconcerned about transience. One may think that Cupitt is now beginning to run out of steam, but these comments must be viewed in the light of his linking of "democratic philosophy" with the Kingdom theology that has appeared in *After All*. His emphasis is now to bring "heaven to earth," and to insist that one's *only* task is to find religious happiness in the here and now. "Last" in *The Last Philosophy* is not intended to mean "final" or to suggest the creation of Cupitt's own grand elitist philosophical system following Plato or Nietzsche. Rather, as he explains in 1998, it signifies that "a very long detour" relying on realism is "now over" and philosophy returns to its original *raison d'être* of debating how best people might live in this world (which is our *last* and only one). In like manner, he uses *last* to mean "the only" in describing the world: "this is the world at the end of the world, the world that has no beyond, the *last* world."

Cupitt argues that metaphysical evil (finitude and transience) is, and always has been, underestimated as a problem by philosophers of religion. To liberate people from the fear of death, transience, and finitude is a great boon. Cupitt aims to bring liberation by telling people to embrace the very thing that they fear. Most religions and philosophies recommend a path that points *away* from this fear, and the realism they advocate prohibits people from completely enjoying their existence. Worse yet, it promotes spiritual slavery by placing over them authoritarian figures who insist on the glories that are "beyond" and a better world elsewhere.

Again, it is the anti-realist vision of life that is at the heart of Cupitt's philosophical system. To be free from realism is to be free to accept life in all its abundance, for anti-realism teaches "a democratic metaphysics of ordinary life [that] attempts to liberate people from the belief that there is something structurally wrong with this life of ours."[36]

For Cupitt, echoing *After All* and anticipating *Solar Ethics*, that is exactly the Kingdom theology that was exemplified by Jesus' Sermon on the Mount. He admits that even in a book principally concerned with philosophy, he still cannot avoid theology. In an Appendix he again appropriates Schweitzer's picture of Jesus as a failed Jewish prophet of the Kingdom of God, arguing that ecclesiastical Christianity quashed Kingdom theology because it was too subversive. Kingdom theology is not grandiose or "fatuously optimistic," but is rather the return to ordinariness foreshadowed by Wittgenstein's turn to ordinary language from 1935 onwards.[37] Of late, Cupitt has adopted a similar depreciation of academic philosophy and theology, preferring the radical nature of "ordinary language"

> In our time we . . . know that there is no reality greater or more primal than the world of ordinary language and everyday life; there is no other world, no higher or more privileged point of view and nothing better yet to come. Where we are is the centre of the world and the place of creation. Ordinariness is ultimate and outsideless; that is it, and there is no Beyond. To say that the Kingdom has come, then, is simply to say that we now recognize that everydayness is all there is.[38]

In short, Cupitt advocates a Kingdom theology without any lofty, idealist claims. It accords with his concern for democratic religious humanism that is created in and through transactional ethics. Such a program opens the way for loving this life by plunging oneself headlong into it — solar living.

Solar Ethics (1995)

Since *Solar Ethics* will be comprehensively covered in volume 2, this survey will be relatively brief.

In the closing paragraphs of Chapter 4, *After All* had given a hint of what Cupitt's next move would be. Using the metaphor of the sun burning itself out, he draws an analogy between the sun and the expressivist humanist ethical way of being, proposing that "we should live as the sun does...it simply expends itself gloriously, and in so doing gives life to us all." The sun also epitomizes an integrated "be-ing" of both life and death.

The sun gives "life" to our solar system, yet at the same time it is dying because "the process by which it lives and the process by which it dies are one and the same." The sun is thus a moral example of how we should live — giving out warmth and love to others. We should not be anxious or cautious, but burn brightly in recklessness and extravagance. This has been seen especially in the lives of many artists, composers, social reformers and scholars who have expended themselves in the service of others. As Richard Holloway eloquently remarks:

> We could let ourselves be ignited by the same recklessness that lies at the heart of the Universe, challenging us to live adventurously, not to be held back by our fears and limitations, but to burn with joy that we are rather than we are not. . . . Meditation on the majestic energy of the universe should increase our love for humanity, should widen, not narrow, our hearts.[39]

Ethical expressivism or naturalism is, as one reviewer states, "a cavalier attempt to cut the Gordian knot of the 'is/ought' dilemma" with the ethical and human life being synonymous.[40] Cupitt provides a version of ethical constructivism that aids people in the re-creating of both themselves and the world in the wake of modern nihilism and existential despair. There are, of course, no answers to specific dilemmas or ethical problems that beset the world. For example, the reader will search in vain for a statement as to whether abortion is right or wrong. Cupitt's radical agenda is not aimed at specifics, but at the generality of "a way of living or stance in life that will lead to the highest happiness there is to be had." This, as the emphasis on Kingdom-theology in *The Last Philosophy* has shown, is deliberately short-term and admits of no long-term goal to which everything is moving. Moreover, the specifics will be worked out in the company of others, since morality is "a matter of *ethos*, something shifting, human, untidy, democratic and transactional, like language."[41]

Cupitt's avoidance of "the Truth" makes him wary of ethical edicts from on high. Yet, despite this, his pragmatism is not visionless, nor does it resemble the caricature of postmodernism as a child set free in the candy shop. Solar ethics is linked to a kind of religion that combines both ecstatic immanence and active re-creation of the world with people expressing themselves by dying in selfless love. Written specifically for members of the Sea of Faith Networks, *Solar Ethics* is an extremely important book since it marks another stage in "the coming out" of Cupitt as well as individuals in the Networks (a second Network in New Zealand has by this time been established). Cupitt confidently urges Network members to put on "a good show" in ethically responsible human lifestyles. Indeed, the original title for *Solar Ethics* was "Good Show," a phrase Cupitt foreshadowed in *Creation out of Nothing* (1990) with his proposal that people should live "a kind of abstract religious performance-art." People are the performance and the show that they put on. There exists no Idealist or Utopian state of affairs that people can work towards; rather everyone and everything is be-coming by the show and "life performance" that they put on. There is no second chance in the hereafter. Like the sun, humans are "pure act."

A significant milestone is reached with the publication of *Solar Ethics*, for now the radical agenda is not solely concerned with the de-objectification of God and the defense of that position, but it has moved beyond all the old distinctions created by realism. Cupitt declares that he is now "post-realist," and he is much more confident and forceful in proclaiming his message. The deliberate use of "queer language" in the book issues a challenge to the members of the Networks for them to "come out" and creatively express ethical religion without God. Having reached the age of sixty, Cupitt discards the vestiges of circumspection and invites others to do the same. The strategies of evasion and deception of *Radicals and the Future of the Church* are replaced by a passion for self-expression. David Hart recognises the provocative nature of the book and its implications for those in the Networks:

> The sun has no interior world, but commits itself in its elipses (*sic*) and eclipses to the process of "coming out" and so defining to all who would see it how it is. . . . Here after the intellectual arguments of Don's previous books we have an attractive and compelling symbol for what all of us in the Network ought to be about. No more hiding under bushels, (but) out and about creating and re-creating our highest ethical ideals.[42]

After God (1997)

Originally entitled "Religion after the Gods," *After God: The Future of Religion* continues Cupitt's post-Christianity and the Kingdom theology of *After All*. It contains three sections:

1. an historical perspective as to why people relied on a concept of God and how de-objectification occurred;
2. how the expressionist, aestheticised view of religion has come to be; (and)
3. the role religion might play in the future.

As I trust this book has shown, these three headings also recapitulate Cupitt's own journey from reliance on an objective God, through subjectivity and mysticism to the fires of Nietzschean nihilism, to embracing linguistic naturalism and the aestheticisation of religion. And of course his antirealist philosophy undergirds the whole project of creating religion without God.

Cupitt addresses the formidable issues of why, and in what manner, people should embrace *any* religious attitude in postmodernity. If, as the philosopher Lyotard maintained, the grand narratives of religion have ceased to have credibility, what possible role could there now be for religion? Cupitt outlines and then rejects the four prevailing rationales for preserving religious beliefs and values in postmodernity:

- *Religion can survive as values* — e.g. family values and moral values that are inviolable. Cupitt dismisses this because in postmodernity all values are free-floating.
- *Religion can survive in the private or domestic realm* — e.g. Orthodox Jewry. Cupitt notes that postmodernity threatens such groups with disappearance or assimilation.
- *Religion can survive as personal faith within the sphere of individual subjectivity* e.g. Kierkegaard, Bultmann and Christian existentialists. Cupitt admits that his early 1980s Christian non-realism was a version of this argument; but postmodernist thought has propelled him into a language-formed public life. Culture now precedes nature.
- *Religion and eternal values can survive in the form of a counterculture* e.g. fundamentalism and New Age cults. Cupitt points to the postmodern truism that there is nowhere to drop out to; your protest against the system remains part of the system.

Cupitt argues that all these approaches simply try to ignore postmodernity when one should welcome postmodernity and redefine religion in terms of it. Indeed, he boldly claims that the postmodern project had its origin in theology, the subject in which people "first found reason to wonder how human descriptive language can be thought of hooking on to or encompassing its topic." So he reiterates his position:

> Unlike the secular theologies of the 1960s, (postmodernity) will "aestheticize" religion, in the sense that it sees religious living in terms of artistic practice and symbolic expression. As redefined here, religious life is an expressive, world-building activity through which we can get ourselves together and find a kind of posthumous, or retrospective, happiness.[43]

Cupitt's religion of the future will be discussed extensively in volume 2.

After God, then, contains most of Cupitt's concerns of the 1990s — "solar living," "ecstatic immanence," "aestheticism," "anti-realism" etc., but sounds *three* new notes. The first, reworking Nietzsche's "innocence of becoming," is the establishment of "religion that is free of illusion, untruth, and power worship." This is, in effect, a correction to the cosmic terrorism that Cupitt finds within Christianity, especially in the way that he and some of his supporters have been treated by various opponents. Second, Cupitt uses postmodernity's emphasis on globalization and transnationalization as a reason to think that non-realism might become the global religious outlook. This is another way of expressing his metaphysic of "cosmic humanism" in *The Last Philosophy*. Linking the ideas of an innocent religion and a world religion, Cupitt ponders the possibility of "a new globalized *world* religion that does *not* work by dividing humanity into a We and a They, but expresses an emergent collective consciousness of the unity of the whole human race with our common world?"[44] Third, he implies that the Sea of Faith Networks might be a beacon of that global religion. This interpretation is not lost on a radio interviewer; but Cupitt remains cautious, answering her that "Sea of Faith itself is unsure whether it is going to go for a global spirituality or to transform the old traditions."[45] In the most significant declaration so far of the Sea of Faith Networks, he puts some of its members in the spotlight as those who "believe in a non-realist reading of Christianity." The intertwining of the theory of the future of religion with how it might be put into practice is now part of the radical agenda, and Cowdell's assertion in 1988 that "Cupitt's will never be a popular religion" appears increasingly doubtful.[46]

In 1996, after twenty-three years as a lecturer in the Cambridge Divinity School, Cupitt decides to take *early* retirement. One commentator remarks that the real reason for his resignation was his feeling "that his colleagues were not taking him sufficiently seriously."[47] This is absurd! While Cupitt might have been disappointed by his fellow academics, their lack of respect for his views did not influence his decision to retire. Rather, ill-health and his desire to continue writing unencumbered by teaching responsibilities were the main reasons for his retirement. Indeed, Cupitt had already begun to scale down his public commitments. And he could have spent his retirement years actively pursuing his passion for chasing rare butterflies across the moorlands of England, but his real motivation was "in order to study and write full-time." Cupitt's fascination with butterflies is perhaps cognate with his emphasis upon contingency

and transitoriness. The fleeting transience of a butterfly's life combined
with its sheer beauty resonates with Cupitt's radical agenda. Butterflies
will adorn the front covers of the three *Everyday Speech* books.

Thus from 1996 onwards Cupitt begins to write even more freneti-
cally, the output increases and he begins to average two new books a year!

Mysticism after Modernity (1997)

A book on mysticism might at first seem a curious place to complete
a survey of expressionism. Yet *Mysticism after Modernity* extends the discussion about the possible nature of religion without God by returning to
the Christian mystical tradition. Cupitt argues that instead of being premodern "psychic sensitives," mystics were postmodern deconstructors who
wrote "their way and ours to a condition of personal religious happiness
that can dispense with traditional ideas of God." Indeed, for Cupitt the
mystics were non-realists steeped in an apophatic tradition marked by a
great blurring of theism and atheism. Instead of portraying the mystics as
orthodox medieval sages, we should see them as radical Christians who
have much in common with the religious radicals of our age (which is
"after modernity").

Cupitt's argument is that religious experience for postmodern
Christians is "the mysticism of secondariness." Having been criticised by
Mary Warnock for advocating "galloping...and destructive relativism" he
counters by declaring that "...relativism is (sort of) true and I *like* it." He
maintains that the mystics were relativists who embraced relativism
enthusiastically. Expanding on the equation of Kingdom theology with
returning to ordinariness, he changes the metaphor to the mysticism of
secondariness, but the effect, is still the same, as this passage indicates:

> The older "platonic" kind of mysticism was usually claimed
> to be *noetic* — by which I mean that people saw religious experi-
> ence as a special supernatural way of knowing something Higher
> that was itself correspondingly super-natural. . . . But now, with
> the end of metaphysics and two-worlds dualism . . . we should
> give up the idea that mysticism is a special wordless way of intu-
> itively knowing the things of another and higher world. . . . The
> mysticism of secondariness is mysticism minus metaphysics, mys-
> ticism minus any claim to special or privileged knowledge, and
> mysticism without any other world than this one. We now get
> . . . that feeling of eternal happiness, not by contrast with, but
> directly off everything that is merely relative, secondary, derived,
> transient, sensuous and only-skin-deep. We have quite forgotten

the old hunger for what is basic, rock-solid, certain and unchangeable: we are content with fluidity and mortality. . . . Relativism should not be a bogey to us: it is true, and religiously speaking it is good news. . . . Why shouldn't we just give up the idea that there's something wrong with being secondary and fleeting?[48]

Here is the nub of the argument. Mysticism is not a form of noesis or contemplation of the supernatural world. There is nothing beyond the world of language, and words such as "spirituality" and "religious experience" refer to the experience of being human. The mystics should be regarded not as word deniers but as wordsmiths. What differentiates them from other writers on theology is their subversive intent; their being writers of protest against institutionalized churches and hierarchies (many mystics being women), and writing poetry (much of it being erotic). Thus, mystics were far different from the way they are portrayed today as "presenters of immediate experience"; rather, "mysticism is protest, female eroticism, and piety, all at once, in *writing*."[49]

Cupitt then reiterates what he had affirmed in *After All*: that religion is able to come to grips with the ambivalence of existence that is felt by everyone. No mystical experience need precede putting that experience into language, but

(as with) St John of the Cross . . . the very composition of the poem was itself the mystical experience. . . . Writing is redemption; religious experience is self-expression in religious art. . . . A person "has a religious experience" when she is able through religious imagery or ritual to "get herself together," and to experience the harmonization and reconciliation of the various forces bearing upon her and within her.[50]

Here Cupitt's interpretation of St John of the Cross brings out fully what had been implied earlier in *The World to Come*. There he had indicated that there was only emptiness beyond the external world of phenomena. In *Mysticism after Modernity* he declares that the mystics teach deification, because the creature and Creator are one. It is this teaching that got the mystics into trouble and made them subjects of persecution by the religious authorities of their own day. Cupitt also employs his trump card, playing Meister Eckhart against the foremost French postmodern writer, Jacques Derrida. He challenges Derrida's interpretation of Meister Eckhart in *Writing and Difference* as one who was "concerned with liberating and acknowledging the ineffable transcendence of an infinite existent" by arguing that Eckhart was a thoroughgoing "non-realist." It is a skilful maneuver, showing that even the most celebrated "saint" of post-modern thought does not overawe Cupitt.

Like Deleuze, as he acknowledges in *The Last Philosophy*, "I find myself obstinately misreading writers from the tradition...to discover where I myself am trying to go." Deleuze's most celebrated or "notorious" re(mis)reading was in *Nietzsche and Philosophy* (1983), in which he argued that Nietzsche's "becoming" was an active force that would overcome nihilism and become the creative force of Dionysius. The "will to power" is not about seeking power but giving and creating — a program of salvation that transforms the reactive forces of *ressentiment* and bad conscience. Deleuze is writing against a neo-Hegelian dialectic interpretation of Nietzsche, and inviting his readers to join in a common project (yet not an Hegelian synthesis) in which "multiplicity, becoming and chance are objects of pure affirmation." This is part of what has been labelled the "new Nietzsche" and Cupitt follows the way of this philosophical movement by using the tradition to his own ends. It is also highly significant that his discussion on Eckhart leads to what will be his next book and stage of thinking — the turn to Heidegger. With the gift of hindsight, one can recognize that Cupitt now digresses from expressionism into "being:"

> *Esse est deus* is Eckhart's formula; Be-ing is God. Here, I suggest, we should (with Martin Heidegger perhaps) locate Eckhart's idea of God. Be-ing, life, the outpouring play of secondariness in the Now-moment: that is as close as language, or we, can ever get to God. . . . We experience everything, totalized into the Now-moment; eternal happiness in the solar efflux of pure contingency. All eternity, here and now. . . . All we have to do is to get our own relation to existence right. Just get on the leading edge of the Now-moment and wait very still and attentive, until you find yourself beginning to surf it. . . . Eckhart has found a way of writing religious happiness.[51]

Cupitt's exploration of expressionism has led, during these seven years, to a position of the "mysticism of secondariness" as a vision of the world where "*all there is*" is the dissolving of the "I" into the continuum of meanings. He suddenly realises that this is what Heidegger calls "be-ing" or "e-vent," "which is (roughly) all existence seen as continuous temporal process, as Becoming or Forthcoming." That be-ing is, of course, not a Being, but *Dasein* and what Cupitt calls "life." The flowing project takes another twist; and Heidegger becomes a tool to aid further exploration.

Stage 5

The Turn to Be-ing & Heidegger
1998

The Religion of Being (1998)

Cupitt's turn to the controversial German philosopher Martin Heidegger occurred in 1998 with the publication of *The Religion of Being*. Cupitt maintains that the essential thrust of his writings — whether described as "democratic philosophy," "expressionism" or "the last philosophy" — has always been *religious*. In short he has tried to "describe the religion of someone who is thoroughly democratic, but who nevertheless goes on wanting to express cosmic yearnings and feelings of love, worship and gratitude; someone who still longs for personal wholeness and redemption, but who cannot find it whilst living under authority."[1] This has led him through the *via negativa* to "active non-realism" and solar living. However, this "final position" was a somewhat inappropriate solution, since it left unanswered the oldest question of philosophy: "What does it mean to be?" Cupitt has thus shifted from his earlier insistence on the "sign" and "communication" which was "the true universal stuff, in which and of which everything is constructed" (*The Long-Legged Fly*) and returned to the traditional starting point of philosophy. And the search for a religion of Being has naturally led to Heidegger.

Having been appropriated by both deconstructionists and Christian existentialists, the granddaddy of existentialism seems to be "the flavor of the month" in philosophical circles.[2] At the same time, however, an attempt has been made to reignite the "Heidegger was a Nazi" controversy first stirred up by Hans Jonas in 1964. The evidence strongly suggests Heidegger's political and ideological leanings towards National Socialism, but commentators vary widely on the degree to which his political views can be distanced from his philosophy. The respected

British philosopher-theologian John Macquarrie takes a cautious approach by emphasising the philosophical appeal of Being; Hugo Ott in *Martin Heidegger: A Political Life* and Victor Farias in *Heidegger and Nazism* argue that before reading any of Heidegger's works, one should be fully cognisant of his warped political affiliations. Heidegger's "silence" concerning the Nazi regime, and his famous refusal to answer the poet Paul Celan's "hope today, of a thinking man's coming word in the heart" after the poet's journey to his mountain retreat at "Todtnauberg" would seem to lend credence to this theory.[3] Perhaps Thomas Sheehan's two articles in *The New York Review of Books* sound the appropriate note of warning to any would-be advocates of Heidegger:

> After the war, holed up in his cabin in the Black Forest, Heidegger wrote: "He who thinks greatly must err greatly." . . . We now know how greatly he "erred." The question remains about how greatly he thought. The way to answer that question is not to stop reading Heidegger but to start demythologizing him.[4]

Cupitt twice alludes to Heidegger's "flawed" past. Both references are fleeting and suggest that he supports the "let's admit the Nazism; but rescue the philosophy" approach. In his "Prosopography" of 1995 he remarks that "in platonism the philosopher has to be personally virtuous, but in these post-platonic days, not all philosophers [i.e. Heidegger] are good people, alas."[5] More damning is the fact that three years later he skirts around the "Nazi" debate: after calmly admitting that Heidegger was "badly flawed by cowardice and worldly ambition," he offers the excuse that "this is the twentieth century (and) we are all of us compromised."[6] The mildest possible retort would be that compromised is one thing and **seriously** compromised is another. However, in order to understand Cupitt's position we should remember that one of his philosophical assertions is extreme short-termism. In *After All*, for instance, he states that "we cannot appeal to History" or to "any great tidal Purposive movement in things [for] everything melts away...We cannot even be sure that our own moral standards will remain unchanged." This induces him to support the decision of two families to drop their concerns as to which of their fathers was implicated in aiding the Nazi oppression of Jews in Holland. "Too much remembering poisons the soul," Cupitt urges. But this begs the question of whether one can — or may — simply forget *after an interval of time* the evil deeds committed by despots and those who helped perpetrate such crimes? Perhaps Cupitt is doing no more than reflecting what has happened politically as tyrannical rulers are shunted around the world, provided 'safety in exile;' or never made to account for their misdeeds. Moreover, what one regime denounces as an act of terrorism, another government hails as fighting for freedom. Cupitt's (and many others') "forgetting" is close to Heidegger's "silence."[7]

At any rate, this criticism of Heidegger's philosophical ideas would not greatly distress Cupitt, because his concern is not to subject them to an "academic" study, but to use them as a foil for his own. The "turn to Being" was not forecast by many, and even caused consternation to those of Cupitt's supporters who thought that he had reached a conclusion with solar living. However, Cupitt explains that by 1994–1995:

> I could see that a further change was taking place, the turn to Being. I had become perhaps too locked into my own terminology. Encountering Heidegger and employing some of his very craftily-chosen vocabulary might help me to be better understood: certainly it has helped me come to a partial synthesis, or inconclusion.[8]

The fruit of Cupitt's thinking is *The Religion of Being*, which becomes an extension of expressionism in that he is trying to forge an idea of what it means to be "religious" in the context of postmodern ideas. Admitting that by inclination he is more of a "subtractor" than an "adder," he understands that "it is not enough simply to talk negatively about non-realism: a new sort of ontology or theory of Being is needed." As with most of Cupitt's appropriations of philosophers and theologians, *The Religion of Being* uses Heidegger's ideas with wild abandon; it is in effect a "deviant reworking" of him. Cupitt justifies his action by saying that he is following the examples of Nietzsche, Bloom, Deleuze, and even Heidegger himself in encouraging deviant readings of texts. Postmodern writers are opposed to "orthodox critical-historical scholarship," and "strong misreading" is a legitimate tactic that is now "widespread."

Those who approach *The Religion of Being* anticipating a learned exegesis on the (more) abstruse parts of Heidegger's (later) corpus will be, as one reviewer comments, "somewhat disappointed."[9] Cupitt himself describes Heidegger's writing as "obscure" and is "sometimes *with* him and sometimes *against* him." He considers most academic interpretations of Heidegger to be "incomprehensible," though he does single out Stanley Rosen's *The Question of Being: A Reversal of Heidegger* as a good interpretation. For Rosen, Heidegger's assertion that reflection on Being serves to "illuminate our experience of beings" should be reversed, since "the more we meditate on Being, the less we see of beings."[10] Unlike Plato, Rosen suggests, Heidegger removes philosophy (or "genuine thinking") from "everyday life." Thus his philosophy cannot avoid "double nihilism": i.e., "the nihilistic attitude towards the world of things and a nihilistic release-ment toward the clearing and the emergence-process."[11] Like Cupitt, Rosen wants a return to "this world," and interestingly argues that Platonism is not a metaphysics of aspiring after a better world elsewhere, but "only a better version of this world." Indeed he argues that "ordinary people" readily recognize this fact and do not need to return to ancient Greece or "only a god" of Germanic folk religion by which to model their lives. Cupitt would concur with Rosen's aim, but would disagree with his interpretation of Platonism. And, unlike Heidegger, he is not "scared" of having to tackle nihilism.

Cupitt's main concern is to write *after* Heidegger, who supervening Nietzsche's "death of God," attempted to create a new vision of the human condition — one that recognized the loss of realism, metaphysics, and transcendence without dissolving into the nihilism that entrapped Nietzsche. This was exemplified in Heidegger's famous statement that "we are too late for the gods and too early for Being. Being's poem, just begun is man (*sic*)."

Here is Cupitt's starting point; for his aim, as Sheehan advises, is to "demythologize Heidegger." Not wishing to end up with an ontotheology of Being, he dispenses with much of Heidegger's theorizing on the history of Being, concealment etc. By denuding Heidegger, Cupitt is preparing the way for the central theme of such later works as *Letter on Humanism*, *Introduction to Metaphysics* and *Time and Being* — namely Heidegger's well documented "turn(s)" away from phenomenological analysis to the lan-guage of poetry to describe "Being." It is at this point that Cupitt inter-prets Heidegger's Being to mean:

> pure groundless fleeting contingency, already passing away even as it arrives, which is why Being does resemble God in allowing us only to see its "back parts." Capital-B Being is being that is prior to any determination, pure transience. It cannot be described in language and it cannot be grasped in thought; but it is always presupposed by language, and it sustains language. It gives itself to us, and it emerges within language. We know noth-ing but the field of view, the field of our own experience. This field is differentiated by language into a field of Be-ing in beings. So Being comes out in our world, the world of language, the only world.[12]

This "move" has perplexed Cupitt's followers. After decades of propound-ing the "language-constructs-reality" thesis, Cupitt seems to be returning to a metaphysical position with Being *prior* to language. Later in the book he equates Being with "non-language" and also writes of Being as "under erasure." But what exactly does this mean? How can one access non-language if language is all there is? Is Cupitt being just as ambiguous as Heidegger? More important, what is "non-language" if language, as Cupitt has insisted for a decade or so, is outsideless? Is he recommending that we revert to some kind of non-linguistic cognitive realm?

The answer is resoundingly in the negative. What has happened is that Cupitt has begun to feel ensnared by his own position, and he has recognized that the sum of an object is more than a person's description of it in words. The seventeenth-century philosopher René Descartes first aired this when he argued that our perception of the world differed from what the world was really like. Descartes solved the dilemma by positing the power of God as implanting in the souls of humans the seeds of the absolute truth of the world. Obviously unable to repeat Descartes' "error," Cupitt resorts to "non-language" and Being (under erasure):

> On non-language, *everyone* seems to find the point hard to grasp. I've argued that all our thinking is transacted in language . . . Therefore all our apprehension of the world is language-mediated. But in that case what's the difference between a *complete description of* A and A's *actual existence*? We can't say in words, so we use the non-words "non-language" or Being (under erasure). Being (under erasure) is prior to the distinction between Plato's timeless Being and temporal becoming. So it may be written as Be(com)ing. It is the indescribable, gentle, constant-yet-only-contingent forthcomingness of everything. Being (under erasure) gives itself to language. Being (under erasure) is not a thing, not even a proper noun, but it deserves religious respect . . . It is not an Almighty Lord, as God was. It is immanent and ubiquitous. It supports our language as hot air supports a balloon . . . we do indeed need a sort-of-idea of something out there beyond all the equations; but it must remain indescribable and purely immanent.[13]

Cupitt's fundamental assertion here is that we should concentrate on Being's function, not its content. We respond to Being as Becoming — that is, to the awe and wonder of the cosmos and of who and what we are as human beings. We respond to the continuous coming into being of the new and novel, whether evidenced by good or evil deeds. Gordon Kaufman expresses this well in his phrase, "the 'serendipitous creativity' manifest throughout the universe."[14] We respond or defer to the forth-

comingness of everything whether we use Paul Tillich's "ultimate concern" or Kaufman's "serendipitous creativity" or such other terms as "cosmic forces" and "historical trajectories and powers." For Cupitt, this is the
same as "Being as Becoming." The responding or deferring to the *function*
of Being as becoming is religion.

Being then is Be(com)ing; and the object of religion is coming to
terms with what it means to simply accept contingency, groundlessness —
or as Buddhism would have it, "Emptiness." Thus religion is "the ordinariness regained." This is where Cupitt departs radically from Heidegger,
arguing that for Being to deserve religious respect it must remain purely
immanent. In an illuminating passage Cupitt summarises four answers to
a "religious response to Being." He admits to having used them all in his
writings, but now wishes to dismiss three of them.

The first derives from Schopenhauer and the early Wittgenstein
(especially in his *Tractatus*), where coming up against the limits of language one enters the realm of the ineffable or mysterious — "whereof one
cannot speak one must be silent." This, as I have shown, is found in the
negative theology of Cupitt dating to 1982 (*The World to Come*). Cupitt
completely rejects this approach when he argues in *Mysticism after
Modernity* that there is no mystical realm and nothing after which to
aspire.

The second answer is that given by the later Wittgenstein in his
return to ordinariness, where religious language and imagery are used to
regulate or guide people's actions. Whether or not there is an objective
God is now irrelevant, and an extreme Kantian position can be adopted.
Cupitt describes this as an "*émigration à l'intérieur*," a stance evidenced
also by those who choose a return to "quietism" or "religious nostalgia."
That is now *passé*, for old religious imagery cannot do the same work
today. Cupitt is discarding his own advice of the 1980s that the word
"God" can still be retained and be used as a metaphor for "one's highest
religious values." Likewise he rejects the notion he expressed only a year
previously in *After God* that sometimes one can slip back into old forms
of prayer "because it helps."[15] He also has concluded that it is morally
iniquitous to pretend that this imagery, with its realist emphasis on living
under authority, represents how things really are in postmodernity. It is
time to shake off such notions.

The third answer is Heidegger's program of "mythicizing" Being so
that it becomes a substitute for the God who is now dead. Cupitt argues
against those theologians who have interpreted the early Heidegger of
Being and Time as a proponent of secular existentialism, which he calls a

"demythologized version of the Pauline account in the New Testament."[16] Rather, Cupitt argues, Heidegger's Being is so this-worldly that no room is left for a metaphysical God — even if, as he concedes, this is what the later Heidegger might have had in mind. Perhaps Cupitt is referring to *Der Spiegel's* interview of Heidegger, "Only a god can save us," in which Heidegger links Being with "the appearance of the god" which will save humankind from the present age which is confronted by global techno-logical disaster.[17] Who or what this "god" is has been the subject of much speculation, but the emerging consensus seems to be that a form of national socialism, rather than any metaphysical God, is at the root of Heidegger's supposed mysticism.

Cupitt prefers the fourth one, in which he reduces religion to "*applied* philosophy, 'edifying' philosophy, philosophy appropriated and lived." This approach paradoxically reunites religion with the ancient philosoph-ical endeavor to create meaning by asking ultimate questions: "What is Being? What is the world? What are we? How is it with us? How should we live?" And thus it is that the religion of being not only encompasses but unites many of the themes of Cupitt's expressionist period; moreover, Cupitt's applied philosophy will avoid Heidegger's fall into nihilism, tri-umphing in resurrection by embracing this (the only) world:

> One is devastated by Being's utter gratuitousness, emptiness, transience; its joyful solar affirmation even as it rushes into obliv-ion. . . . The death of the self thus brought about by the *Seinsfrage* then leads unexpectedly to an extraordinary sense of deliverance and happiness, which has been described as "ecstatic imma-nence." It is a queer reverse-resurrection. One is raised from the death of illusory belief in another world, back into the truth of this world, now fully understood and accepted for the first time. It is a resurrection not into an imaginary other world after death, but back into this world, into "glory."[18]

Cupitt's whole emphasis on responding to Being is predicated on the understanding that people need something to respond to. It is a version of the celebrated argument that if there were no God, it would be necessary to invent one. Interestingly, responding to "something around us" sepa-rates those who are religious from those who are not. The religious atti-tude can save, whereas irreligious humanism cannot; and for Cupitt, as we have seen, religion is the means of overcoming nihilism. In a reversal of the Cupitt of the 1980s, and especially the autonomous stance of *Taking Leave of God*, he states a new conviction:

> The religious person is a person who feels that none of us is, or can be, wholly autonomous, self-made and monarch of all he surveys. There is at least something that one must defer to . . . something that we surf, something with which we are interwoven. . . . Human living is always highly situated. . . . We are never wholly alone. We are always embedded in and related to something we need to acknowledge. By contrast, the anti-religious person says we should regard every injunction to defer to something or other as politically suspect . . . It is better not to accept any antecedent limits to our freedom and our responsibility.[19]

So, Being (under erasure) is "there" (also under erasure!) to facilitate celebration of contingency, flux and solarity — Cupitt's radical agenda. That is why he considers the book "a sort of poem in praise" of Being — even though, like Heidegger, he can't say *exactly* what that is. The difficulty lies in the fact that Being is not something or nothing, but is continually being brought forth — be(com)ing — by creative living. This offers far more than Nietzsche's bleak aphorism from *The Will to Power*, that "becoming aims at nothing and achieves nothing." Rather, becoming is in the dance of language, which can offer unifying metaphors and stories that show how good and how beautiful the world can be. The world is open and indeterminate, with endless creative possibilities; and religion should be like a "midwife of Being," bringing forth new life to people.

In a too-easily-overlooked Endnote in his next book, Cupitt indicates how he has arrived at his idea of Being. An article in *The Scientific American* disclosing a new doctrine of modern physics that updates Heisenberg's uncertainty principle, has influenced him. According to this finding "a vacuum isn't a pocket of nothingness [but] it churns with unseen activity even at [absolute] zero, the temperature defined as the point at which all molecular motion ceases."[20] Cupitt argues that there is a parallel with his philosophical thought. If there is still quantum fluctuation even at supposed absolute zero, then there is no absolute reality (Being) or absolute nothingness. "[I]nstead, there is everywhere wobbling, fluctuation and a dance of probabilities." The old theological realist maxim that *ex nihilo nihil fit* (nothing can come into being out of nothing) is repudiated, and with Darwin we can assert that everything has arisen by chance "out of minute fluctuations in the void," and hence without the necessity of a Designer. Just as virtual particles can flash into existence from the energy of quantum fluctuation, it is now possible to create *ex nihilo*. Cupitt's radical agenda has now rendered unnecessary the long struggle to overcome nihilism, for there is no such thing as absolute nothingness, absolute void, or absolute anything. Rather, everywhere is the trembling dance of possibility out of which the world comes, as one speaks (i.e. via language) — this is Being (under erasure), Be(com)ing. With this important insight Cupitt can escape from the fear of the Void into the postmodern O-Void (Cupitt's own coinage from ovoid), which leads to the feminization of metaphors and religion. The masculine, realist language becomes softened, and following the lead of such French feminist writers as Luce Irigaray and Julia Kristeva, he can restore feminine images in order to overcome nihilism and declare that "from the womb of time, the O-Void, the *chora* . . . out of nothing, a stream of pure contingency pours forth unceasingly, like a well-spring or fountain.[21] Being thus takes on a degree of femininity, and Cupitt can find a temporary resting place that can "cheer him up." Unlike Heidegger, he does not fall into nihilism, for the religion of Being is continually pouring forth, revealing that there never can be absolute nothingness. Nihilism is embraced *and overcome*.

The final chapter of *The Religion of Being* was originally an autobiographical note to be used elsewhere should Cupitt's continuing health problems necessitate his abandonment of writing. Its addition makes *The Religion of Being* the most self-revelatory of all of Cupitt's books and even offers a glimpse of what he thinks may have been the goal of his writing. True to his self-deprecating way, however, he disclaims his own understanding of his literary accomplishments and rejects the status of guru. Indeed, everything in Cupitt's radical agenda is open to re-negotiation. He has distanced himself from institutional churches and has handed back to his Bishop his licence to officiate out of disgust at the hierarchy's treatment of his Sea of Faith colleague Anthony Freeman. However, he retains his Anglican orders and communicates weekly at his local college Chapel. He favors the "religious democracy" of a group like the Society of Friends and wonders whether the Sea of Faith Networks might be the "first church of the future."

The implications are clear: we ourselves will create the new religion of being because each one of us is rest-less and a world-builder; but at the same time the restlessness must be tempered by Heidegger's insistence on knowing how to "dwell." This tension between active non-realism and a kind of Zen minimalism with a meditational discipline to "attend" becomes the subject of his next book.

The Revelation of Being (1998)

Because his advancing years and academic retirement permit a greater sense of freedom and the necessary space to reanalyse his work, Cupitt's later writings take on a more personal and even cathartic tone. He is perhaps the last person one would expect to have experienced "visions," but he admits that they have occurred at regular intervals throughout his life.[22] Indeed we are surprised to learn that his turn to Heidegger was an attempt to make sense of these extraordinary mental awakenings.

One special "revelatory" vision occurs in July 1997 as he meditates (hence the front cover of the book depicts Cupitt in his study at Emmanuel College overlooking Parker's Piece, the famous parkland area in Cambridge) on what he has written in *The Religion of Being* concerning the forthcoming of Being:

> We give up everything and suddenly find eternal happiness, on the surface only and just Now, where Be-ing pours quietly forth into the dance of meanings and the flickering play of the most transient phenomena. That's bliss; it is "the mysticism of secondariness," and it is what I am here calling the Revelation of Being — joyous acceptance of the way everything turns out, or just happens to be. It is high-speed ravishment. . . . It is what Carlyle calls "natural supernaturalism." It is eternal happiness, briefly, in and with the here and now.[23]

Here he is advocating a rapturous attention to the passing moment when we realize and acknowledge that this life is all there is and we must love it now before it ceases to be; it is, as Richard Holloway explains, no different from what poets and artists have been advocating over the centuries: "All art is trying to get us to pay attention, to look at life and love it before we go from the fire-lit banqueting hall out into the winter's darkness."[24]

Cupitt's vision is of a secular Trinity — the co-extensiveness of Language, Man, and Being. However, unlike Heidegger who in his opinion still enforces an "ontological difference" between Being and beings, it is with Being, Man and Language as co-workers. Thus he exclaims that he has experienced a Heideggerian "Ereignis" (an event of Appropriation). This is an "oh-so-transient beatific vision of the outsideless, living and purely contingent three-in-one and one-in-three unity of Being, Man and Language." Philosophical bliss is attained "by jumping not out, but back in; not ecstasy but entostasy." In short, it is "a purely immanent, *for me*, living, moving unity of everything."[25] This same idea appears in *The*

Religion of Being, where he defines outsidelessness as "the coincidence of humanism and nihilism; (and) anthropocentrism is, non-viciously, *all there is*." The aim of the book is to explain this brief neurological event and to further elaborate the religion of Being. Thus, *The Revelation of Being* might be read as an appendix to, or expansion of, *The Religion of Being*.

Cupitt's "Ereignis" is thus totally immanent, non-metaphysical, and epitomized by the "frivolous coinage" — entostasy — which means to "jump back into ourselves" and accept the world. This does not entail a Nietzschean *amor fati*, a blind acceptance of whatever befalls us (for which Cowdell criticised Cupitt in 1988), but exults in the knowledge that we are *also* the co-creators of our world.[26] We must be responsible for the fate of the Universe, our own lives and the lives of those around us. There is an ethical dimension to Being:

> I do want Being for what may be called ethical and religious rea-
> sons. It is our needed complementary Other. It slows us down,
> stabilizes us, settles and situates us. It represents to us, and indeed
> it is, our life's pure abyssal transience, which sometimes makes
> me sick with metaphysical horror but at other times moves me to
> intense love. It makes me feel solar.[27]

The religion of Being is not quietistic acceptance but calls us to coura-
geous action against all that would harm the joy and beauty of life for others.

Cupitt's own "slowing down" is not a result simply of advancing age and ill-health, but also of his religion — which is, as he first outlined in *After All*, both active and contemplative. The Religion of Being is both restlessness (actively creating the world) and an attendance to the joy of living in the present moment (the forthcoming of everything). It is in this tension of what might be and our human fear of nihilism (i. e. the awareness of death, transience, and nothingness) that the secular Trinity of Man, Language, and Being operate co-extensively.

In a final section entitled "Words" Cupitt admits that the key to understanding *The Revelation of Being* is "anthropomonism." This is not a new word for Cupitt, who used it as early as 1985 in *Only Human*. He argues that he is following a line of argument put forward by one of the most revered conservative Christian theologians, Karl Barth. By focusing his theology on Jesus Christ, Barth made it "christocentric" (Christ-cen-
tred). His critics seized on his apparent adoption of a doctrine of "chris-
tomonism" — the insistence that all knowledge of God was restricted to

what was revealed in Christ. So where Barth posited "christomonism," Cupitt places "anthropomonism" — the doctrine that "Man" is the foundation and organising principle of his philosophy.

By "Man" Cupitt means "the human realm, (which) incorporates the whole known and language-traversed world; and then (he) empt(ies) out the human self." Cupitt admits he does the same thing with "Language"—and, I would suggest, "Being." In other words, Being, Man and Language are metaphors of the human condition of temporality, contingency and forthcomingness. One can start with whichever of the three one chooses; but one ends (or re-starts) with immanentization, which is "the passing show of existence," and the dance of probabilities. Cupitt concludes with almost evangelical fervor: "And I truly believe that the Love of transient, contingent Being which has come upon me in my later years is a religious advance upon the Love of God which so filled me from 1952 until 1978 or thereabouts."[28]

This is the revelation of Being, and he regards it as the polar opposite of his long-time adversary — the religion of realism and absolute power, which is defended at all costs by official religious organisations. By way of contrast, Being is gentler and lighter, and so deserves religious respect. The revelation of Being does not warn people against the evils of life, but invites them to be "at home" in this world, to treat it with respect, and to share it with others. This is the religious object that we should love, although since most religious people are realists, it is what they most fear and seek to escape. From the religious suicide bomber to the holy crusader, religions have licensed innumerable acts of insanity that have promised the perpetrator a better world elsewhere and eternal rest in the arms of the Almighty. This is the religion of "death," and as such is in stark contrast to the revelation of Being, which is the religion of life. This becomes the subject of his next book and takes us into his next stage — the focus on ordinary language.

Ordinary Language

1999–2000

The New Religion of Life in Everyday Speech (1999)

Cupitt ended *The Revelation of Being* with the suggestion that the whole of our postmodern experience is a kind of secularized religion. This is nowhere better revealed than in ordinary language, which he sees as the most profound source of philosophy. Cupitt anticipates the thesis of *The New Religion of Life in Everyday Speech* when he remarks upon David Pears' interpretation of:

> Wittgenstein's "subtle positivism" (or "quietism") in being ready to admit that in the end we cannot do better or know more than what's already open to everyone in ordinary language and everyday life. And I would make the same point: philosophers and religious writers must give up any pretensions to be some kind of gnostic or seer who has found the way to a Higher Truth. All such claims are bogus. Ordinariness is abyssal. Nothing in all philosophy can surpass the subtlety and beauty of the most ordinary English idioms.[1]

Refusing to accept the label of "gnostic" applied to him by some commentators, Cupitt points out that his philosophy of life is one that ordinary language and hence ordinary people already recognize. He is not propounding anything different from what people now actually *say* that they believe. It should be acknowledged that in this book Cupitt is doing what no other theologian has done before. The methodology that he employs is radically new. He proposes a novel, empirical method that has far-reaching implications for both the study of "academic theology" and the religious thought of the future. Instead of looking back to the "classic" texts and authoritative figures, he argues that the theologian must attend closely to the way language is changing, and needs to listen to the way the *Zeitgeist* (spirit of the times) is moving. This has been forced on theologians because religious language is nowadays scattered throughout reports of ordinary experience. To find out what people believe we should take note of the way that language is changing.

Cupitt collects more than one hundred and fifty phrases ("ordinary English idioms") that contain the word "life," and that capture the philosophy of life that has been encoded into common speech during the last few years of the twentieth century. Cupitt admits that his selection cannot be all encompassing, urging readers to send him any "Life idioms" that he has omitted. He also concedes that the emergent philosophy of life could be to some degree culture-bound, but then his central argument has been that language encodes cultural meaning(s)!

The life-idioms connect with his radical doctrine that the objective God is now dead, having been replaced with a new religious object — "life." Democratic philosophy, following Wittgenstein's later emphasis on ordinary language, turns out to be the best radical theologian. Rather than adopt the oft-quoted view that there has been a steady secularization of religion, Cupitt offers a different interpretation: what has happened is the *sacralization* of Life. Despite frantic and often violent efforts by religious fundamentalists, we have witnessed a shift in religious vocabulary from God-centered to Life-centered. This can be easily shown, for example, in the subtle changes that have taken place in a Western funeral service. The new emphasis on *this* life has transformed the way that many Christian clergy conduct funerals, as evidenced by the common practice of replacing the sermon with a eulogy. Spoken by a friend or relative, the eulogy focuses on the "life" of the deceased, rather than what happens in a future life. The role of the clergyperson is reduced to that of an officiant instead of the main practitioner. The latter traditionally preached to the bereaved family concerning the "miseries of this sinful world" and commended the soul of the deceased to God's everlasting arms. This change of emphasis could be seen in the very public funeral of Diana, Princess of Wales, in 1997. The major thrust of the memorial service was a celebration of her life and a thanksgiving for all that she had accomplished on this earth, with her brother giving the eulogy and a popular entertainer,

Elton John, singing a song "Goodbye England's Rose" (a rewriting of "Candle in the Wind"). There was no mention of a future life and it was left to the Archbishop of Canterbury to attempt to bring an "eternal" dimension to the service. In Western countries the distinction between religious and non-religious funerals has become increasingly blurred, with many families choosing civil or other non-religious celebrants to conduct funerals services for their loved ones.

Cupitt considers that "life" for most people now takes on all the attributes of the "lost God," and is worshipped in much the same way. The book is less a new departure than once again a change of metaphor. Instead of an engagement with the obscure Heidegger as to what is meant by "Being," Cupitt explores what is meant in everyday speech by "life." It is a Wittgensteinian retreat from academia combined with an attempt **not** to be restricted to a particular vocabulary. Cupitt is (as he tells his followers to be) like an artist creating many images to give a new slant to his form of expressionism. He reveals his hand when he says:

> After I had completed the Being-books it struck me that if I changed my vocabulary again and rethought everything in terms of the relation to Life, I would find that ordinary language has already done most of the work for me. Instead of the usual struggle to communicate ideas that normal people find deplorable, I'd be in the happy position to say: "Look! This is what you are already saying; this is what you think." Isn't it?[2]

Simply put, where Cupitt's scheme invokes Being, ordinary language posits "life" — not only biological life, but also human social life in the "life-world." As we have seen Cupitt is not afraid to use other thinkers to his own ends. Just as he was inspired by Karl Barth he now turns to the existentialist German-American theologian, Paul Tillich, taking his cue from Tillich's use of the word "theonomous" in his *Systematic Theology*. Tillich wanted to find a way beyond autonomy and heteronomy to describe the individual self united with God, the ground of being. Cupitt likewise wishes to find a stance somewhere between autonomy and heteronomy, having rejected the autonomous individual (the Enlightenment project failed) and being cognisant of the postmodern emphasis on heteronomy (the claim of another over the self). Accordingly, he coins the word "bionomous" to describe the religious objectification of life. It is not unreflective thinking, but "a postmodern, highly conscious, elective or *chosen* immediacy," standing between autonomy and heteronomy. The central tenet of bionomy is that "in very recent years many or most people have at last become able to say a religious Yes to biological life and their own mortality."[3] This obviously concurs with the post-Christianity he has been promoting as "solar living," and the coextensiveness of this life and the outsideless world.

It must be re-emphasised here that Cupitt is not retreating into a form of fatalism that tells people to accept the often tragic circumstances of life that result from birth or ill fortune. Cupitt has not abandoned his active non-realism and insists that people must create a better world for themselves and others. As I shall show in volume 2, there is a cutting edge to Cupitt's ethical (solar) living and religion that can answer such critics as Leslie Griffiths, who object that many third-world people "would not even care to get to page two of this book."[4] Cupitt's main preoccupation here has nothing to do with supporting the oppression of ethnic minorities by authoritarian governments, but with demonstrating how in Western democratic countries the demise of "God" has been replaced by the sacredness of "life." Indeed, it may be countered that in third-world countries realist notions of "God" have often been responsible for the suppression of indigenous peoples. Indicative of the often reciprocal relationship of missionary activity and colonial expansionism is the celebrated remark of South African Archbishop Desmond Tutu: "When the white man arrived we had plenty of land and he had the Bible…[Then] the white man taught us to pray, and when we opened our eyes, we had the Bible and he had the land." While some missionary organizations are now much more "culturally aware," and some early missionaries performed noble and caring work, indigenous peoples often were (and worse yet, sometimes *still are*) regarded as "primitive," both religiously and materially. The underlying message of many religious organizations has been that *only* by adopting a Christian realist understanding of God could "the natives" be "saved" physically and spiritually. Far from a guarantee of emancipation from authoritarianism or slavery, Christian realism was and often is quite the opposite.

However, the main objection to Cupitt's argument here is not from liberation theologians but rather involves whether his argument accords with what ordinary language is saying. As Gregory Spearritt points out, the book itself contains a contradiction to this bionomous thesis. Cupitt also acknowledges that people might say they want to live their own life, but as yet only a few really mean it. Most are content to idolize others, and so become believers, fans, and spectators in a way that makes them fit only for vicarious life. Thus, "pessimism about our life remains religious orthodoxy."[5] The evidence from sociological data — for example, the high rate of youth suicides — suggests that many people have yet to follow Cupitt in affirming *this* life.

Has Cupitt then led his readers on a wild-goose chase with a claim he cannot really substantiate? In a remarkable conclusion, Cupitt himself offers a critique of his own argument by proposing that the English language contains many "it" and "It All" idioms which could equally be the religious object. Moreover, as will become clearer in his next book, "it" and "It All" are more in tune with the pessimistic attitude to life. Whether unwitting or deliberate, Cupitt's contrast of the theologian Dietrich Bonhoeffer and the poet Samuel Beckett in the final paragraph of the book sets up the two religious "positions" that can be found in ordinary language — affirmation of life and fear of "It (All)." Bonhoeffer, despite his imprisonment by the Nazis in the Second World War, could still write positively about life and being alive, whereas Beckett enjoyed "freedom" but was a life-denier.

Cupitt's experimental religious writing impels him to find out what "It (All)" might *mean* when used in everyday speech.

The Meaning of It All in Everyday Speech (1999)

True to his ironical postmodern spirit, Cupitt originally entitled the book: "Read all about it!" However, he admits, "I never really expected to get away with such a title." His second excursus into Wittgenstein's "This language game is played" stems from his interest in the way ordinary language pictures us surrounded by an 'it' that we must try to fend off. The radical agenda of Cupitt has led to the postmodern condition with the dissemination of religious language into what was once deemed to be secular language. "It" now evokes five emotional responses:

1. Something *unmentionable* — e.g. dirt, feces, money — improper subjects of conversation.
2. Something *unspeakable* — often linked with sexual activity.
3. Something *unnameable* — inhuman or monstrous — arouses fear/disgust.
4. Something *inevitable* — can't be changed or influenced.
5. Something *ineffable* — represented by images of vast emptiness/the abyss.

This "it" becomes "what we are up against," the dark side of Jungian analysis, the tragic side of life and bad dreams. "It" passes into "It All" when "it" becomes the cosmic dark side that people either try to avoid or fight against, and is given names like Necessity, Fate, Destiny, God, Chance, Nothingness, and Death. The resulting dilemma is whether people should avoid, *or* resist, "It All."

Cupitt's recent religious writing has resulted in both acceptance of what is and an overcoming of this same situation. It is no surprise, then, to find that his analysis of "it" language is both an acceptance of what was expressed by Being as Be(com)ing, and a struggle to make sense of "It All." First, Cupitt recounts how he has had sleepless nights pondering two idioms — "the way of it" and "it came to pass." The fruit of his insomnia is that he can "say now that the mystery of It-all is the mystery of Being, which is the mystery of Its way of coming and passing."[6] Here is another linking of the acceptance of the outsidelessness of existence and its expression in ordinary language. Second, in his two *Everyday Speech* books he cleverly shows that by affirming the language of "life" one can conquer the nihilism of "it" and "It All." Pessimism gives way to affirmation of life. In fact, he goes one step further than this in wondering whether the "it" side can be forgotten with the result that people simply accept and joyously affirm life whatever befalls them. However, he immediately has to retract that thought because ordinary language still uses "it."

The layout of the book in twenty-eight almost Nietzschean sections reminds one again of the "unsystematic" nature of Cupitt's radical agenda, which is "to explore new territory." He tells his readers that he is not trying to convince them of his position, but because language is phatic and emotivist, is simply expressing what language says and feels. The "Life" and "It All" books describe the religion of the 1990s: they affirm "life" yet still deeply fear the encircling darkness that is part of (human) existence. Cupitt's vision is that if one can say "No!" to the "It All" and "Yes!" to "life" (especially in the sense of biological life), then this is the religion of radical Christian humanism and the post-Christianity begun by Jesus. This vision too can be found in the "Kingdom" language of ordinary speech and will be the subject of his next book. For now, Cupitt very deliberately challenges his reader to tell him he has got it all wrong. The implication is that one must use language to do so; and ordinary language, as he has demonstrated, will back him up, for that same ordinary language expresses the common world as we have come to experience it!

Kingdom Come in Everyday Speech (2000)

The third and final book of Cupitt's trilogy of "ordinary language theology" is again concerned with advancing the hypothesis that ordinary language is the "best radical theologian," and that the views he has been espousing, although ridiculed by his opponents, are *already* an inherent part of our daily communication. The three books have been produced separately but they should be read as one volume expressing "the religion of everyday speech."

In this book Cupitt is particularly interested in the degree to which the traditional religious eschatology found in the New Testament has been "realized," or made actual, in ordinary postmodern language. Thus, his aim here is to show how far secular postmodernity is a fulfillment of what he considers to be the original message of Jesus — the Kingdom. In a typical Cupittian move (following Kierkegaard) he makes another "sharp" polarization, this time between Kingdom theology and Ecclesiastical theology, identifying nine differences:

Ecclesiastical Theology	*Kingdom Theology*
world to come	here and now
God is transcendent	God is immanent
mediated by priests/scriptures	immediate/intuitive
credal and dogmatic	visionary
hierarchical	egalitarian
one Tradition/Canon	global
mysterious	explicit
discord	one equal music
sacred versus profane	all on same level

Ecclesiastical theology contains the realism that Cupitt so much detests (hierarchy, authority, dogmatism), while Kingdom theology expresses anti-realism (immediacy, creedlessness etc.)

He then takes up the theme of *After All* by proposing that secular postmodernity has "realized" much of this Kingdom theology. But before his critics can seize on a simple equation of "postmodernity = the Kingdom," Cupitt insists that it is rather the case that postmodernity "hints" at what Christianity should have be(come). In short, postmodernity has to a large extent "realized" what Christianity should have been. The Church was meant to be only an "interim" organization. Once it regains an interest in Kingdom theology, it will release its grip on realism and "pass out" into a post-Christianity that is "democratic" and radically humanistic.

Central to Cupitt's thesis is that postmodernity is an era (the *last* era) characterised by radical humanism and humanitarian ethics. These are the two important "signs" that the Kingdom Jesus foretold has arrived. For Cupitt, Jesus really did equate religion with humanitarian ethics, and "faith in God" with performance of the traditional "works of mercy." By this Cupitt means both that God is dispersed into humanitarian acts of love and justice, and that secular postmodernity has *already* recognised this. He charts the historical progress of radical humanism within Christianity, locating its origins in the Middle Ages (*circa* 1065) and especially in the shift of devotion "from God to the suffering of a fellow-human being" (i.e., the figure of the crucified Jesus). Although for traditional Christianity acts of humanity were always "conditional" — their ultimate aim being to increase one's own chances of eternal salvation — humanitarianism, which today has become an acceptable word, is postmodernity's working out of that radical humanism. Once the "death of God" has been embraced then "God" becomes dispersed into ethical concern for needy people "irrespective of race, colour or creed." He mentions the situation in 1999 of Albanian Kosovars who, despite being Muslims, were defended by Western Christians against their Serbian Orthodox (Christian) attackers. Thus, humanitarian ethics are a good indicator of how the Kingdom might have already been "realized."

Combined with this is Cupitt's view that postmodernity is the *last* era. The use of *last*, as when he used it in *The Last Philosophy*, does not mean "final," but rather in the sense of "only this" ("and no other"). Here Cupitt is indebted to Nietzsche's idea that people are living at the end of or *after* history. He often states that postmodernity is the time when people live *after* history: "the world at the end of the world is a world after history," or simply "the end of the world." By using this apocalyptic style of language, Cupitt suggests that people in postmodernity have accepted the demise of all the realist organizations and traditions that once frightened them into belief or coerced them into obedience. In an important Endnote he explains:

> My talk of "history" as the period during which people groan under the regime of great disciplinary institutions is of course derived from Nietzsche. The ones he has chiefly in mind are pretty much the same as the ones I've groaned under: the state, the church, the army, the university.[7]

This neatly allows Cupitt to reintroduce one of his key expressivist themes of the 1990s — the figure of the solar artist or performer. One who lives *after* history is no longer constrained by the moral frames of the past, but "seeks moral liberation by making an exhibition or show of the self." Being freed of the superstitions of the past, the solar performer creates meaning and helps to build a better world by *burning* and pouring out in self-expression. This is vintage Cupitt, but just as one begins to think that he has got stuck in a rut, he yet again sounds a new note. In *Kingdom Come in Everyday Speech* he introduces the figure of "the selfless professional" to counterbalance his solar performer. He has noticed that in postmodernity the "gradual secularization of social action" has led away from the "condescending amateur" to the selfless professional:

> Today, the kind of person who is ethically most admirable is an *unperson*, a person without what everyday speech calls an "identity": he's a soldier in a blue beret on peace-keeping duties, a person working for *Médecins sans Frontières*, a professional negotiator, or an "aid worker." And it is this cool, beliefless, identity-less and very postmodern sort of saint who has made the word humanitarian respectable at last.[8]

This is a very profitable move for Cupitt. He can counter those critics who might have viewed the solar artist or performer as some sort of self-indulgent bohemian by combining solar ethics with humanitarian ethics and thus, as I will discuss fully in volume 2, reconciling "personal" and "social" ethics.

Through most of *Kingdom Come in Everyday Speech* Cupitt is extremely up-beat and optimistic about postmodernity and how it exhibits many facets of the Kingdom. Postmodernity is *the* time (*the only* time) in which the religious hopes of a more democratic, more humanistic, and less oppressive era symbolised by "the Kingdom" are becoming fulfilled. As he did in *The New Christian Ethics*, he urges everyone to add his or her bit of human love to make the world a more loving place in which to live.

But just as one begins to think that utopia has nearly been reached, Cupitt becomes cautious. He anticipates the critics who claim that he is being naïve about the excesses of our contemporary capitalism; or that he is "denying (or at least playing down) the manifest evils and injustices that are everywhere" and that markets need regulators to keep them from falling into the hands of unscrupulous power-brokers. Although he rejects the validity of these criticisms, he is confronted by the postmodern paradox of being "torn between a highly optimistic and a darkly pessimistic view of the postmodern human condition." It might appear an abrupt closure, yet it resonates with the main thrust of his flowing project of the past twenty or so years. Cupitt ends as a hopeful prophet of *this* world, insisting that by a combination of solar self-expression and humanitarian social ethics we can (if necessary) change it:

So there is nothing left for religion to be except a complete and whole-hearted commitment to this world which is the last world. Of course it is not without evil and suffering, but it's all we've got, it is all ours and it is all there is: so we must make the best of it. Got that?[9]

But how can it be done, now that church Christianity is in decline? What resources can one call upon? Cupitt's next book attempts to extract religious "teaching" from the philosophical anti-realism that he has been expounding for the last decade and that will help people make the best of *this* world.

Stage 7

The Religion of the Future

2000 to date

Philosophy's Own Religion (2000)

Cupitt remarks that *Philosophy's Own Religion* is "a summary of [his] own final outlook." However, we should be wary of such statements. He admits that he has had a few previous "final outlooks," and there may be more to come!

Philosophy's Own Religion is both a new departure and a summary of the direction that his endorsement of expressionism has taken since 1990. It reprises a good deal of *After All*, *The Last Philosophy*, *The Time Being* and the *Everyday Speech* books, with Cupitt renewing his call for a religious humanism that has no fear of "the big bad wolf of nihilism." Indeed, he neatly sums up the central concern of the book by drawing a contrast between himself and the British "radical orthodox" theologian, John Milbank:

> Milbank thinks that philosophy by itself drives towards and ends in nihilism, from which we must escape, and do so by accepting divine Revelation; whereas I say that philosophy ends when it comes at last to ordinary language's own philosophy — which turns out to be very much what religion has called kingdom theology.[1]

Milbank, formerly a student of Cupitt, together with a group of mainly Cambridge University theologians, has formed a movement known as "radical orthodoxy" to combat what they see as an insidious tide of secular reason and all thought which brackets out God. Following François Lyotard's ground-breaking insights of the late 1970s, Milbank welcomes postmodernity as a time when the metanarrative of secular modernity comes to an end, but he refuses to accept that this is to be replaced by a plethora of small narratives (*les petit recits*). Rather, post-modernism is embraced because it can give way to something greater than secular reason, a metanarrative that can supplant or "out-narrate" it: namely, the Christian Gospel. For Milbank there is only one alternative — either the Christian story (specifically an Augustinian reading of the Church as the City of God and a realm of ontological peace) or nihilism. Indeed all other narratives and ideologies — whether secularism, scientific truth or Enlightenment humanism — are versions of nihilism. Thus for Milbank any ideology that attempts to exclude God is nihilistic by definition. All postmodern narratives must now be informed by the Christian story and acknowledge their participation in the transcendent. If they do not, then they are nihilist and must be a form of necrophilia — a philosophy of death. Adopting the medieval paradigm of theology as the "Queen of the Sciences," radical orthodoxy argues that theology *alone* can absorb and make possible all other discourses, for only theology can save the world from nihilistic despair and damnation. Unlike postmodernism, which preaches depthlessness, Milbank urges people to trust the depth behind things, a depth that is not the nihilistic abyss enjoyed by Cupitt, but God.

Gavin Hyman correctly observes that here we have two competing frameworks — "linguistic textualism" and "radical orthodoxy" — that refuse to acknowledge each other's existence, since both offer an either/or scenario. In the case of Cupitt it is either antirealism or realism. For Milbank it is either God or nihilism. When both combatants have clearly staked out their respective positions, no common ground exists:

> Thus, nihilist textualist theology embraces the death of God, the advent of nihilism, the end of theology and the birth of a/theology, whereas radical orthodoxy embraces the return of God, the overcoming of nihilism and secular reason, and the rebirth of theology.[2]

Hyman calls for "moving through" these either/or combatants by using the insights of the French philosopher-theologian Michel de Certeau to embark on an "endless exodus of discourse." The either/or is replaced by a neither/nor, with people dwelling neither in Milbank's (Augustinian) City of God nor in Cupitt's "fully present," but in an intermediate zone between the two. Hyman appropriates the figure of the "outlaw" who wanders in and out of the known landscapes of postmodernism, nihilism, and theology without being captured by any of them, but is free "to raid and return." We do not choose either Milbank or Cupitt, he announces, but "move through" both their territories and leave a space or clearing for the "other."

Although he would reply that Hyman wants to "have his cake and eat it," Cupitt would seem to have to make a choice — and yet there is not really a choice, because people have *already* opted for anti-realism. This philosophy is revealed in the way people express themselves in their ordinary everyday speech. Everyday language is committed to a particular vision of the world, and currently that vision is anti-realism, as can be seen, for example, in today's use of the word "perception" to mean interpretation. Cupitt explored our current philosophy in ordinary language in his *Everyday Speech* books and now he analyzes it extensively in Part 2 of this book. In contrast to much of the Platonism of academic scholasticism (excluding American neo-pragmatism and French post-structuralism), ordinary everyday language is anti-realist. It is time, following Wittgenstein's advice, for academics to take note of what people *say* (i.e. believe)! Rather than suggest with Milbank that nihilism must lead to a situation of despair because it denies God and therefore, like the postmodern cyberspace and themeparks, promotes a materialism that is "soulless, aggressive and nonchalant," Cupitt proposes (Part 3) that from anti-realism one can extract "teaching" that is the basis of the religion of the future.[3]

Cupitt now becomes much more positive in outlook and answers those critics who accuse him of being interested only in deconstruction. He adopts an almost Buddhist approach to setting out his *dharma*, although he prefers the English phrase: "The Teaching." However, it is obvious that his long acknowledged endorsement of Buddhist spirituality has influenced him here. The teaching is set out in seven concise chapters with a brief summary at the end of each one. The teaching supplies *principles* that empower a non-dogmatic religious outlook:

- Religious meaning has become dispersed across culture in everyday language and the religious/secular distinction has been erased. The whole of life is religious.
- Life is outsideless and we should commit ourselves unreservedly to our own transient lives.
- Salvation is found, not by withdrawing from the world, but in expressive, solar living.
- Life and death are not polar opposites but are always mingled. Life involves the awareness of the closeness of death.

- Humanism and humanitarian ethics are expressions of a new global religious way of life.
- Ecclesiastical Christianity is to be replaced by informal religious associations, which emphasize sharing one's story and Kingdom values.
- There is no absolute religious object, but there are valid religious attitudes towards Be-ing.

Cupitt has thus solved the problem he confronted in *After God* — the lack as yet (in 1997) of a global religious vocabulary.[4] Having now identified teaching that can begin to cross religious and cultural boundaries, he is ready to accept that the distinctive features of the various local faiths may be nothing more than materials for the heritage industry. He echoes this by arguing in a paper presented at the Sea of Faith U.K. Conference XIII (2000) that around the world all the great surviving monuments of the old religious culture are now being taken over "by the Heritage industry, which will lovingly restore and preserve them, unchanging and dead." He has thus moved on from his earlier advice in *After God* that one can still follow one's own local religion.

It can be seen, then, that Cupitt's flowing project has brought him to a point where he looks *beyond* the churches for the religion of the future. The new note that is sounded in this book is his admission that his writing is "not addressed to the church (but is) for me and others who think as I do."[5] Allied to this is his endorsement in Part 1 of globalization as a force for good, in that "religious (and ethnic) differences get less and less important."[6]

It is obviously a contentious assumption, and it meets fierce criticism even by some within the Sea of Faith Networks. Yet, as I have shown, Cupitt is simply following on from his thoughts in *After God* and *Kingdom Come in Everyday Speech*. Moreover, his "global" teaching is now very similar to that outlined by his Antipodean non-realist friend Lloyd Geering, who sets out the negative impact of globalization but admits that it is "a process that cannot now be held back."[7] It also provides great opportunities to end destructive regional tribalism, Cupitt argues, and offers the possibility of creating a global consciousness that will make people themselves responsible for the survival of the cosmos. Avoiding any discussion of the negative impact of globalization, Cupitt prefers to argue for its benefits. Both Cupitt and Geering view globalization as a religious vision that has its origins in the Judeo-Christian tradition, especially in the concept of the Kingdom of God. This emphasis on the Kingdom and his turning from the churches point towards Cupitt's next book, *Reforming Christianity*.

Reforming Christianity (2001)

Cupitt is now forced to find a different publisher as the once radical theological printing press in the United Kingdom that had welcomed his writings since 1971 (SCM Press) changes editorship and becomes less reformist. England's loss is America's gain as Polebridge Press takes up the mantle and becomes his publisher. This switch also helps to widen Cupitt's sphere of influence. In stark contrast to the neglect of the British academy, the importance of his contribution to the advancement of religion is widely acknowledged. Fittingly, he is inducted into the Order of D. F. Strauss and becomes a Fellow of the Westar Institute, joining a group of more than two hundred Fellows who include Karen Armstrong, Marcus Borg, Lloyd Geering and John Shelby Spong. Indeed, Cupitt's flowing project is something that fits easily with Westar's twofold mission of fostering collaborative research in religious studies and communicating the results of the scholarly study of religion to a broad, non-specialist public. Furthermore, Cupitt's thirty-year project of democratising religious ideas mirrors the work of Westar's founder, Robert Funk.

Funk's aim in establishing Westar was to make accessible essential knowledge about biblical and religious traditions that had been hidden away from the general public, often encoded in the specialist jargon of universities and seminaries. We have seen also in Cupitt's journey that such research is often considered too controversial or too complicated for lay persons to understand. Fearing open conflict or reprisal, scholars commonly talked only to one another. Likewise, the churches often decided what information their congregations should be allowed to hear. Through publications, educational programs, and research projects like the Jesus Seminar, Westar has opened up a new kind of conversation about religion and has promoted "the fourth R" — religious literacy. This is an honest, no-holds-barred exchange involving thousands of scholars, clergy and other individuals who have critical questions about the past, present and future of religion. Obviously Cupitt and Westar are well-suited. The Strauss medal is particularly fitting because of Cupitt's own devotion to one he described in *The Sea of Faith* as "an unofficial saint" of those whose critical exploration of faith is not welcomed by official religion, and who are compelled to spend much of their time in exile because they are considered rebels. In the BBC TV Series Cupitt made a poignant trip to Strauss's grave to lay flowers on it. The recognition that Cupitt receives from Westar is long overdue, for his only other academic recognition is an honorary D.Litt, conferred on him by Bristol University, England in 1984. It also reveals that he is gaining a substantial following in North America.

Pursuant to his teaching that ecclesiastical Christianity will be replaced by informal religious associations and networks, the main ideas of this book were taken from four papers he presented to the Sea of Faith Networks at their Conferences in United Kingdom, New Zealand, and Australia in 2000. The current anti-realist religious outlook that Cupitt describes in *Philosophy's Own Religion* is similar to the "religious dream" of the Kingdom in earliest Christianity. Thus, *Reforming Christianity* is the theological companion to *Philosophy's Own Religion*, arguing that people should move on from church Christianity, which is in terminal decline, to Kingdom religion, which is what secularism and globalization are pointing towards. Kingdom religion has four main features:

- life becomes a single sacred continuum
- all value in life becomes intrinsic
- ethics becomes purely humanitarian
- human consciousness becomes fully globalized.

For Cupitt, this also is a way of recovering the message of the historical Jesus — which, as Albert Schweitzer recognized so well, was lost once ecclesiastical religion became established. Cupitt follows Schweitzer in viewing Jesus as a failed eschatological prophet who looked for a new realm to be established on this earth. Rather than carry out his message of an earthly kingdom, the Church deferred its realization to a heavenly world after death.

In Schweitzer, Cupitt returns to one of the prominent "saints" of *The Sea of Faith*, one whom he labelled as "the first post-Christian Christian." Cupitt too proclaims himself to be "post-Christian," pointing towards that religion of the future based on the dream of a Kingdom that is *this-worldly*; that shows the way to religious fulfilment in *this* (and *only this*) life, and which secular culture has (much more than the churches) begun to realize. He demonstrates how that ancient religious dream has been pursued through the United Nations, international law, democratic politics, ceaseless global communication and humanitarian ethics. It is a world now committed to the struggle for the emancipation of women and the reconciliation of ethnic and religious differences. It was left to the secular world, especially in such "events" as Martin Luther King's "I Have a Dream" speech and John Lennon's "Imagine," to tell the story of a "new world" in which people would live together in harmony and re-ignited hope.[8] This is the nihilism that Milbank and other "radical orthodox" savants regard as so dangerous and that needs to be rescued by theology. On the contrary, declares Cupitt — this nihilism is ethical humanitarianism that helps others solely on the basis of our co-humanity "regardless of race, colour, creed, gender, sexual orientation, doctrinal soundness and moral desert."[9] Unlike radical orthodoxy, which reinforces the distinctions between God and man, master and servants, light and darkness, nihilism promotes a world in which everything is on the same level and everything is open and explicit. This is the anti-realist, nihilist, Kingdom vision of postmodern secularism and early Christianity.

This "new" world of ours represents a much more highly developed version of the original Christian programme than anything available from the churches. A religious statement like the Papal Encyclical, *Dominus Jesus* ("The Necessity of the Church for Salvation"), promulgated on 5 September 2000, with its insistence that one religion is not as good as another and its dismissal of non-Roman Catholic ministers' orders as "defective," shows not only the growing conservatism of one of the historic churches, but also its lack of tolerance for views other than its own. It is this authoritarian approach of religious organizations, Cupitt asserts, that ironically has led to the "redundancy of the Church" — with secular culture creating the Kingdom of love that was supposed to have been the work of the churches. In an Appendix to the book, Cupitt includes a letter from a friend who has remained in active ministry in the Church and who argues that the Church does "here and there" manage to propagate Kingdom religion. Cupitt's retort is that in the end ecclesiastical religion must always attempt to define and control and dominate Kingdom theology, and that is why Christianity must be reformed. However, he is ultimately skeptical about whether ecclesiastical religion has the will to reconstruct itself and opines that it will "run true to form and so opt for decline." Again, he looks to informal religious societies and networks characterised by "mutual respect for each other's spiritual freedom" as those that point towards the Kingdom religion of the future.

The "religious" people of the future are those who both endorse globalization as a force for good that overcomes regional tribalism, and also actively work in their own lives to create a more loving and just existence for themselves and for others.

Emptiness and Brightness (2001)

Cupitt admits that he is now writing trilogies. After three books on everyday speech, *Emptiness and Brightness* is the third book on his "final outlook" of the religion of the future. Again the themes of anti-realism, nihilism and Kingdom religion pervade the book, and he endorses the work of "some fellow-voyagers" in the Westar Institute's Jesus Seminar (USA) and the SnowStar Institute in Canada. Radical theology and non-realist ideas have been aired in these centers for the progress of religion. The circle of influence is gradually increasing in size.

Cupitt changes his description of himself from "post-Christian" to "empty radical humanist." By "empty" he means, in the Buddhist sense, impermanent: a thing "consists merely in its own shifting relations with everything else." He proposes that the postmodern paradigm for life is no longer the novel but the soap opera — a story that is told endlessly, "world without end," and is humanistic and nihilistic. There is no conclusion, only (in)conclusions. Religion is not about looking to find meaning in a metaphysical entity outside this world, but to affirm and say "Amen" to this life. Indeed, meaning is now mean-ing — the fictions that we use to bring closure to our world, but which need to be continually reinvented. Mean-ing is a continuous process that is transacted in and through language and it is *endless*. Religion is rooted in ordinary people's experience of life, which is like a great soap opera. The once great religious traditions are, despite the desperate attempts of fundamentalists and counter-post-moderns (Milbank and radical orthodoxy) coming to an end; and people must learn to embrace a world of endless change and exchange. Transience is all that there is and there is no guiding force from beyond. People must **not** seek after another Buddha, Jesus or Yogi, but look to themselves to create meaning (which is ever changing) and embrace the world as it is, unsupported and contingent. This is the teaching that is coming to birth in the new (Second) Axial Age, the vision that is now in the process of demolishing the foundations of the world created by the first Axial Age — the dualistic idealism associated with Plato, and the world religions that arose from great teachers like Buddha, Jesus and Mohammed. People must begin again, and the process is democratic. There is no leader (including Cupitt himself) to unveil mysteries or guide the mass of people in a spiritual direction. Life is here and we must live it by sharing our ideas, and by a humanitarian ethics that we make up as we go along. There are no foundations, only stories that are about everything and nothing at the same time!

Yet this new situation is not one to be feared. For only by passing through the fires of nihilism — much as Christianity proclaims that in baptism believers pass through the fires of death — will resurrection, or what Cupitt labels "brightness," be achieved. Cupitt uses the word "brightness" in exactly the same way that he used "Man" in *The Revelation of Being*. Brightness signifies "the human knowledge and consciousness in which alone the world finally becomes fully and beautifully its own finished self." This is another way of saying that we have to make our world bright by the way we live. In other words, solar living! Cupitt has changed the language and metaphors but arrived back at the same place.

Cupitt admits that from now on his influence will wane and "there will only be some tidying-up operations" because the "main thrust has been taken as far as (his) abilities can take it." The implication is that now it is up to us all to play our part in the creation of the religion of the future. Perhaps Cupitt's own interpretation of Albert Schweitzer in 1984 is still an apposite summary of his "final outlook", as he combines nihilism with radical humanism:

> For Schweitzer, just as much as for atheists like Schopenhauer and Nietzsche, no good purpose is discernibly at work in the course of events in this world. There is no loving heavenly Father looking after everything; on the contrary, the world is a scene of tragic conflict and suffering in which life is alienated from itself. The Christian hero pits against it his own will-to-love, immersing himself in the sufferings of creation, and striving — even though inevitably unsuccessfully — to infuse and transform the amoral will-to-live with the ethical will-to-love.[10]

Conclusion

This survey of the seven stages of Cupitt's radical agenda has shown
not only the breadth of his formidable knowledge of philosophy and theology, but the ease with which he bridges the usual gap between "the academic" and "the ordinary person." His methodology is deliberately
deviant and he uses and abuses scholars to suit his own ends. In many
places, as I have shown, an alternative reading could equally well have
been established. But that, it must be emphatically reiterated, is to mis-
read him and to be side-tracked from the purpose of a flowing project —
one that has been intriguingly, but perhaps accurately, described as
"surf(ing) the cacophony."[1] We have had a bumpy ride on the sea of faith
in the course of exploring a vision of religion, ethics and community in
the light of postmodernity, the end of metaphysics, the advent of nihilism,
and the death of God. Dennis Nineham accurately sums up Cupitt's
endeavours:

> Cupitt has always been an enthusiast, and the leopard will
> not change his spots. Yet he is one of the very, very few theolo-
> gians to be grappling with the issues central to their discipline,
> and surely of vital interest to us all. What is needed is a recogni-
> tion that the style in which he advances his thesis is not impor-
> tant, together with a much more sympathetic and sustained
> engagement with his work than it has so far received.[2]

It has been my intention in this book to provide that "sympathetic
engagement" which, I have argued, was begun by Scott Cowdell, but has
not been significantly advanced since 1988. I have concurred with

Cowdell that from "within his unique perspective on the nature of reality I believe that his theology is consistent," and have shown that his flowing project does **not** result in the presentation of "carefully polished 'final positions.'"[3] Indeed, Cupitt himself, in a response to a charge by Trevor Beeson that his books are "works in progress" rather than "substantial summas," says that "the only *summa* I can offer is the linear series of my books and the fidelity (or otherwise) of their witness to the way the human situation has been changing in my time."[4]

I have also contended that the main refuters — White, Thiselton, Williams and Hebblethwaite — have been interested only in firing "critical realist" salvos warning others to keep clear, rather than trying to understand Cupitt's areas of interest. Likewise, radical orthodoxy's attack on his linguistic nihilism is mounted within an incompatible framework that is both obscure and anachronistic. The postmodern becomes the premodern and there can be no allowance for engaging with the new religious concerns outlined by Cupitt. These I have identified as "ethics," "religion," and the "Sea of Faith Networks." They emerge from this survey as his focal interests and indicate the central themes of my "sustained engagement" in the next volume. In particular, I will concentrate on how far Cupitt's re-evaluation of these concerns is useful to those who wish to remain within the mainstream Christian denominations. Does Cupitt's ethics provide an adequate response to Christian living *after* God? Has Cupitt's radical Christian humanism or post-Christianity broken the ecclesiastical ties, or is there still room for maneuver? What is the role of the Sea of Faith Networks?

But these are questions to be debated in the next book; for now, let me summarise the essential features of Cupitt's flowing project, the discoveries that have taken him from liberal Christian to empty radical humanist. This journey is based on three ingredients.

First, Cupitt is passionate about the necessity for religion and wants to redefine Christianity as religious humanism with "God" becoming "Man." The old transcendent sacred is dispersed into humanity. The divine comes down into the human world. We can see this happening, for example, in the case of Rembrandt. He was a Christian humanist who was much influenced by Jews, and whose painting evinces a religiousness of humanity or human religiousness. It is that sort of religion that Cupitt loves, and which he hopes will emerge in postmodernity. Indeed, at the end of *The Revelation of Being* he suggested that the whole of our postmodern experience is a kind of secularized religion. Today we have secularized Christian doctrine into our common life and our social skills. Cupitt also insists that this new religious humanism can be fully realized only when the old dogmatic religion comes to an end. Moreover, the *only* religious beliefs that are true are the ones that deny the truth of certain other religious beliefs, such as the Buddhist "no self/soul" doctrine (*anatta*). The Buddhist view that the self is just a collection of natural capacities and phenomena is for Cupitt the nearest that one can come to a true religious doctrine. Thus he can be both an unbeliever who rejects all dogmas, and also a practising Christian who attends weekly services. He admits that he uses the Church as a "shell company" or convenient backdrop against which to show up the Kingdom religion he is working towards. He still addresses a predominantly Christian audience because this audience gives him the best chance he has of being heard, and he sees himself fated to become the last ecclesiastical prophet. Moreover, Cupitt considers himself to be a religious inventor — not some kind of authority figure or guru, but a new sort of religious experimenter who produces innovative religious ideas and encourages others to "make a fresh start." Just as the theologian Matthew Fox urges people to embrace an "original blessing," instead of "original sin," so Cupitt's religious inventions often involve reversing customary values and practices. Contemporary religious thought must reassess ancient "truths" about the human condition and the way to happiness, but without recourse to the old assumptions and vocabularies. The "religion of the future" ought to function like an art college: it should be a loose association in which people discover their own creative powers.

Second, Cupitt's journey has led him to embrace a way of living religiously without the need for God — a modality that he labels "expressionism." He has been attracted by German expressionism in art, and by the concept of the self becoming itself by an outpouring of symbolic expression. Accordingly, he has insisted that the essential function of life is to communicate, to express ourselves, and to realize ourselves in a profusion of symbolism. This means that he considers Jesus to have been an expressionist, especially as he is portrayed in the Sermon on the Mount. He admits that the final version of that homily contains two competing and co-existing visions of religion: Kingdom religion that is solar, eschatological and attentive to the *ici et maintenant*; and a more cautious and worldly ecclesiastical religion that in view of the Kingdom's non-arrival has relapsed into organizational structure and dogmatism. Cupitt considers the (more original) Kingdom vision of the Sermon on the Mount as a charter of the expressive living to which Jesus was calling us. And that same Kingdom is the source of inspiration for a new religious world free from dogmatism and the scare tactics of a realism that divides "us" from "them."

Hence he insists that we have to create a world that looks as if it has been produced by love — world-love. Instead of arguing the old way that the world looks as if it is the expression of God's love, Cupitt urges that we need to create a world that looks *as if it is* the expression of *our* love for it. "God" was the original non-realist. God's thought and creative activity produced a world, and now we move into "God's" territory by realizing the extent to which we describe and interpret our world. Creating this secularized version of what was originally thought of as God's activity means we must translate theology into anthropology, and the doctrine of Christ into the doctrine of us. God passes out into self-expression in the world through the action of his Son, thereby creating a gap between Himself and us. Similarly, the only way that you can give yourself is by expressing yourself, thereby creating a kind of gap between the intimacy of your own being and your fullness in symbolic expression. All that which was originally said of God becomes a sort of template for the construction of modern selfhood. We become ourselves by the living of our lives, by going out into expression and passing away. Cupitt wants to retain much of the old theology, but give it new humanistic interpretations and generate a *human religion* out of it. In classical Christianity the human self was a metaphysical substance and a spiritual individual, eternal and immortal. In Kierkegaard the self was a process of becoming, a striving to become; a striving for self-realisation. Cupitt has now a more Buddhist view of the self. The self is a field of energies that are passing away. To become someone is to find a *persona* or a role that one can act out through self-expression. We need to live like artists or actors: we need to say our piece, make our contribution, paint our picture and put on our show. That is Cupitt's expressionism — religion without God.

Third, Cupitt has arrived at a postmodern ethics that he calls "ethical non-realism." There is no ready-made moral order "out there." That idea died as soon as modern science arose through Descartes. Once the world picture became mechanized, the notion of a revealed or discoverable higher Truth had to be discarded. It took philosophers a very long time to admit this, and it was really only with Nietzsche that philosophy expressly said, "We invented the concept of purpose; it is lacking in nature." There is no moral world order "out there." We have got to put in the ethics. Indeed, morality arises the same way as ideas like human rights and values that we recognize as *ours*, and that we know to affect our perceptions. For Cupitt, then, morality has to be continually reinvented and projected like art — which, since the nineteenth Century, has learned to live by reinventing itself all the time. We have to live like that. Cupitt again contrasts the disciplined professionalism of science and the solar expressivism of art. Art reinvents itself, continuously projects itself outward. That is how one should live, that is ethics.

Cupitt's flowing project has thus taken him a long way — from his relatively conservative and orthodox first book *Christ and the Hiddenness of God* in 1971 to the extreme radicalism of solar expressionism and ethical non-realism. His flowing project has consisted of thirty or so years of re-invention. Indeed, his literary project may be seen as a continual self-reinvention and rethinking of his position. Cupitt is not like many theologians who try to defend the same system of thought for as long as they possibly can in the face of academic criticism. For him, trying to produce a philosophical system is like trying to draw the landscape outside a railway carriage window. You are travelling so fast through a changing landscape that you can't get it down quickly enough. The fact that we are temporal means that his work had to take the form it did — for just as we are changing all the time, so is his literary project. Although he now insists that he is "slowing down" and that he has reached a "final outlook" of "empty radical humanism," the story of the seven stages of Cupitt's journey should make the reader reluctant to accepting any closure just yet. He himself cheerfully admits to being like "an old prima donna," who can't resist just one more outing, and one more farewell tour!

Cupitt's project has become steadily more poetical and literary and less formally academic. Indeed, he has become decidedly anti-academic, and with Kierkegaard tends to blame the historical-critical method for the decline of religion. If you teach the Bible and study theology strictly by the historical-critical method, you kill them both instead of living by them and making them exciting. In academia, alas, the emphasis is upon submitting the correct bibliography and the most acceptable scholarship, being able to read Greek and the ancient languages, and conforming to a sort of museum dream of accuracy and objectivity. But, for Cupitt, that is not religious thought — that is death. As a result, he no longer frequents academic circles, but tries to create a religious thought that actually works for ordinary people who are members of "the church and religion of the future" — loose religious associations and networks that are free of dogmatism and open to creative religious thought.

Perhaps it is fitting to close this survey with Cupitt's own description of his flowing project and where it has taken him:

> I am someone who likes modern Western philosophy, who retains
> a strong devotion to Jesus Christ, who has an affinity with much
> in the Jewish and Buddhist traditions, and who has been trying

to build up a body of free and experimental religious writing which may or may not one day be of use to others.[5]

The undergirding argument of this book is that Cupitt's "religious writing" is indeed of "use to others," and much too valuable to go unrecognized.

Notes

Introduction

    1 A question asked by Anthony Thisleton. See, *Interpreting God and the Postmodern Self*, 110.

    2 Crowder, review of *Atheist Priest?*, 302–303.

The Formative Years

    1 Cupitt, *Life Lines*, 92

    2 Cupitt, *The Sea of Faith*, 34–37. See also Cowdell, *Atheist Priest?*, xvii.

    3 Hastings, *A History of English Christianity*, 544.

The Negative Theology

    1 Cowdell, *Atheist Priest?*, x.

    2 Cupitt, *Christ and the Hiddenness of God*, 22.

    3 See R. Williams, "Religious Realism: On Not Quite Agreeing with Don Cupitt," 3–24 and Hyman, *The Predicament of Postmodern Theology*, 44–49.

    4 Cupitt, "An Apologia for My Thinking," 2.

    5 Ibid., 2.

    6 Cupitt, "Free Christianity," in *God and Reality*, 16ff.

Non-realism — "coming out"

    1 Cupitt, letter to author.

    2 See Cupitt, *The Leap of Reason*, ix; and *The Religion of Being*, 158–59.

    3 Cupitt, *Taking Leave of God*, xii.

    4 Derrida, *Writing and Difference*, 146.

    5 Cowdell, *Atheist Priest?*, 19–20. David Edwards reveals this admission was due to "an exchange of letters" between himself and Cupitt in *Theology* in 1981 (See Edwards, *Tradition and Truth*, 84).

    6 Cupitt, *Taking Leave of God*, 96.

    7 Cupitt, *Mysticism after Modernity*, 115. Cupitt's later dismissal of "autonomy" is often not recognized, as evidenced in a recent article by David Cheetham

which attacks Cupitt's "fully autonomous spirituality" without having perceived that this is not the Cupitt of today but of 1980 (see "Postmodern Freedom and Religion," 29–36).

8 Cowdell, *Atheist Priest?*, 64.

9 Thiselton, *Interpreting God and the Postmodern Self*, 107.

10 Cupitt, letter to author.

11 Cowdell, *Atheist Priest?*, 28–29.

12 Cupitt, *The World to Come*, 18.

13 Phillips, "Theological Castles and the Elusiveness of Philosophy — A Reply," 440.

14 Cupitt, *Philosophy's Own Religion*, chap. 8.

15 Cupitt, *The World to Come*, xvii.

16 Ibid., 150.

17 Ibid., 140.

18 Hebblethwaite, *The Ocean of Truth*, 52.

19 Cupitt, *The Sea of Faith*, 2.

20 Cowdell, *Atheist Priest?*, 33.

21 Cupitt, *Only Human*, xi.

22 Tarbox Jr., "The A/Theology of Don Cupitt," 73.

23 Cupitt, *The Religion of Being*, 162.

Postmodernism and Anti-realism

1 Cupitt, *The Religion of Being*, 161. For the partial citation of "getting one's thinking up to date and learning to live truthfully in his own time," see *Life Lines*, 10.

2 Anderson ed., *The Truth about the Truth*, 10. The most celebrated explanation of postmodernism is given in Ihab Hassan's "table" of "characteristics of postmodernism" (see "The Question of Postmodernism," in *Romanticism, Modernism, Postmodernism*, ed. Harry R. Garvin, 123). Hassan traces the origin of the term postmodernism to Frederico De Onis (ibid., 117ff).

3 See Derrida and Vattimo eds., *Religion*.

4 Thiselton, *Interpreting God and the Postmodern Self*, 85.

5 See especially Cupitt's comment that "Deconstruction does not show that a text can mean anything whatever: what it shows is that the author's attempt to express himself unambiguously involves him in making 'logocentric' metaphysical assumptions about meaning and the power of language to express truth univocally...he has to write as if meanings were as clear, hard and distinct as glass marbles; and they are not. Language is a system of differences . . . Deconstruction is a form of critical reading" (*Life Lines*, 194–95). Cf. White, *Don Cupitt and the Future of Christian Doctrine*, 199; and Hampson, "On Being a Non-Christian Realist," in *God and Reality*, 96.

6 Cupitt, *Life Lines*, 214.

7 Cupitt, *The Long-Legged Fly*, 7–8.

8 White, *Don Cupitt and the Future of Christian Doctrine*, 165.

9 Bowker, *Licensed Insanities*, 60.

10 Cowdell, *Is Jesus Unique?*, 267–68.

11 This paper was subsequently published, see Cowdell, "All This, and God Too? Postmodern Alternatives to Don Cupitt," *Heythrop Journal* 33: 267–82. This seminar at Victoria University, Wellington, New Zealand, was part of Cupitt's lecture series in New Zealand sponsored by Victoria University and St. Andrew's Trust for the Society of Religion.

12 Ibid., 279–80.

13 Cowdell, "The Recent Adventures of Don Cupitt," 35.

14 Williams, *Revelation and Reconciliation*, 127.

15 Hebblethwaite, *The Ocean of Truth*, 151.

16 Edwards, *Tradition and Truth*, 286.

17 Cupitt, review of *Kierkegaard and Modern Continental Philosophy: An Introduction*, 530.

18 Cupitt, *The Long-Legged Fly*, 7. This point is also made by Cowdell in "All This, and God Too?" 271.

19 Thiselton, *Interpreting God*, 114 (cf. Edwards' description of the incongruity of Cupitt's position to Cupitt's forthright reply to Edwards in *Tradition and Truth*, 73 [Edwards], 285 [Cupitt]).

20 Cupitt, "Free Christianity," in *God and Reality*, 19.

21 Williams, *Revelation and Reconciliation*, 142.

22 Cupitt, *Radicals and the Future of the Church*, 143. This is the two "negatives" spirituality of Pearse.

23 Cupitt, "A Marginal Note," in *Five Years of Making Waves*, 25.

Expressionism — religion without God

1 Cupitt, *The Religion of Being*, 159.

2 Cupitt "A Marginal Note," in *Five Years of Making Waves*, 24–25.

3 Wilson, review of *The Revelation of Being*, 328.

4 Cupitt, *Creation out of Nothing*, x.

5 Thiselton, *Interpreting God and the Postmodern Self*, 117, quoting John O'Neill, *The Poverty of Postmodernism*, 197.

6 Cupitt, *Creation out of Nothing*, 87–88. Cowdell identifies a few scatterings of autobiographical information in Cupitt's works; for example, his stealing of a chelsea bun at the age of ten and the "religious experiences" of 1953 and 1955 (*Atheist Priest?*, xv–xix). However, it is not until 1998 that Cupitt attempts some discussion of "what (he) was doing," although he claims *not* to "be any sort of expert upon...(his) own ideas" (*The Religion of Being*, 155).

7 Cupitt, *Creation out of Nothing*, 90–91.

8 Ibid., 16–17.

9 Cowdell, "All This, and God Too?", 269.

10 Cupitt, *Creation out of Nothing*, 60ff. He also discusses this event in *The Meaning of It All in Everyday Speech*, 93. For Robinson's struggle with pancreatic cancer see James, *A Life of Bishop John A.T. Robinson*, chap. 8. For the sermon on cancer see pgs. 304ff.

11 Cupitt, *Creation out of Nothing*, 66–67.

12 Ibid., 96–97. For Geering's idea of religion as "superglue" see *Does Society Need Religion?*, esp. chaps. 1 and 3.

13 Cupitt, *The Journey*, 102, as quoted in Pattison, "Non-Realism in Art and Religion," in *God and Reality*, 162.

14 Cupitt, *Is Nothing Sacred?*, xix.

15 Thiselton, *Interpreting God and the Postmodern Self*, 88.

16 Ibid., 150. Cowdell himself admits his own critical realist position: "I conclude that despite its very great appeal, Cupitt's programme and his religion leave enough unanswered questions not to rule out at least a qualified theological realism" (*Atheist Priest?*, xiv).

17 White, *Don Cupitt and the Future of Christian Doctrine*, 98.

18 Cupitt, *What Is a Story?*, 133.

19 Ibid., 154.

20 Ibid., 154.

21 Cupitt, *Radicals and the Future of the Church*, 143.

22 Buddhism is, of course, as diverse as Christianity, taking many forms and shaped by different cultures. As Gregory Spearritt has indicated, Cupitt favors the Madhyamika variety of Mahayana Buddhism (with its teacher Nagarjuna) and the Zen Buddhism of Dōgen ("Don Cupitt: Christian Buddhist?" 359–360).

23 See, Stambaugh, *Impermanence is Buddha Nature*, 24.

24 Cupitt, *The Time Being*, 81.

25 Ibid., 19.

26 Ibid., 142.

27 Spearritt, "Don Cupitt: Christian Buddhist?" 372. Cupitt does return to Buddhism in *The Religion of Being* (1998), but again it is adopted to provide an analogue for his use of the idea of non-realism: "In the region of discourse where Buddhists use the word Nothing, Heidegger uses the word Being, and I have for nearly twenty years used the word non-realism" (Ibid., 8).

28 Cupitt, *The Time Being*, 174.

29 Dawes, *Freeing the Faith*; Hart, *Faith in Doubt*; Freeman, *God in Us*. All these books will be discussed in detail in volume 2.

30 Cupitt, *After All*, 17.

31 See Cupitt, *The Sea of Faith*, 114.

32 Cupitt, *After All*, 50.

33 Ibid., 117.

34 Ward, review of *The Last Philosophy*, 477.

35 Cupitt, *The Last Philosophy*, 121.

36 Ibid., 11.

37 This was shown in Wittgenstein's propensity to urge his students and friends, for example Con Drury and Francis Skinner, to renounce "academic philosophy" and to take up ordinary jobs. One of them, Norman Malcolm, refused to heed his advice to "do some manual job . . . such as working on a ranch or farm" and went on to become a famous philosopher himself. Wittgenstein was something of a reluctant professor who left Cambridge University from 1919–1929, trained to be an elementary school teacher and taught school children in rural Austria.

38 Cupitt, *The Last Philosophy*, 131.

39 Holloway, *Doubts and Loves*, 31.

40 Hey, review of *Solar Ethics*, 394.

41 Cupitt, "Unsystematic Ethics and Politics," 153.

42 Hart, review of *Solar Ethics*.

43 Cupitt, *After God*, xiv.

44 Ibid., 122.

45 Cupitt, interview by Rachael Kohn, *Post-Millennial Prophets; the Spirit of Things*, ABC Radio, 1999.

46 Cowdell, *Atheist Priest?* 73.

47 Beeson, *Rebels and Reformers*, 171.

48 Cupitt, *Mysticism after Modernity*, 8–9.

49 Ibid., 62.

50 Ibid., 74–75.

51 Ibid 100–103.

The Turn to Be-ing and Heidegger

1 Cupitt, *The Religion of Being*, 3.

2 See Rapaport, *Heidegger and Derrida* and Macquarrie, *Heidegger and Christianity*.

3 Celan "Todtnauberg," trans. Hamburger, in *Poems of Paul Celan*, 293. For a scathing attack on Heidegger's political affiliations and the damage that it has inflicted upon his supporters (especially Derrida) see preface to the MIT Press Edition, *The Heidegger Controversy*, ed. Wolin.

4 Sheehan, "Heidegger and the Nazis," 47. For an excellent discussion of the Wolin-Derrida argument see Sheehan, "A Normal Nazi," 30–35.

5 Cupitt, *The Last Philosophy*, 139.

6 Cupitt, *The Religion of Being*, 6.

7 For a defense of the moral imperative for postmodernists (and in particular the "heterological historian") to speak out and to be the "custodian of memory" concerning the injustices of the past see Wyschogrod, *An Ethics of Remembering*.

8 Cupitt, *The Religion of Being*, 154.

9 Hampson, review of *The Religion of Being*, 131.

10 Rosen, *The Question of Being*, 134.

11 Ibid., 273.

12 Cupitt, *The Religion of Being*, 14.

13 Cupitt, letter to author. Cupitt views Descartes' idea of "the power of God" as one more step on the way towards dispensing with God as an "unnecessary hypothesis" (Cupitt, *Kingdom Come in Everyday Speech*, 30).

14 Kaufman, *God – Mystery – Diversity*, 101.

15 Cupitt, *After God*, 85. For a rejection of Wittgenstein's philosophical "quietism" see Cupitt, *Philosophy's Own Religion*, 76ff.

16 Cupitt refers specifically to the work of Brian Ingraffia. The same accusation could be made against John Macquarrie who, despite agreeing that Heidegger is not a theist, nevertheless believes that one might argue: "Being has taken the place of God...In Christian theology, God is love. In Heidegger, 'It gives' is an act of giving or donation, and since he has told us that the 'It' which gives Being is Being itself, then the act of giving is also an act of self-giving, and so not different in any major respect from love" (*Heidegger and Christianity*, 99).

17 "'Only a god can save us': *Der Spiegel's* Interview with Martin Heidegger," in *The Heidegger Controversy* ed. Wolin, 91–116.

18 Cupitt, *The Religion of Being*, 115.

19 Ibid., 137.

20 Cupitt, *The Revelation of Being*, 107–8 n.1 quoting Yam, "Exploiting Zero-Point Energy," *Scientific American* 277, no. 6: 82.

21 Cupitt, *The Religion of Being*, 16.

22 For a retrospective analysis of Cupitt's visions by Cupitt himself see *The Revelation of Being*, 8–10.

23 Ibid., 10.

24 Holloway, *Doubts and Loves*, 245.

25 Cupitt, *The Revelation of Being*, 11.

26 Cowdell, *Atheist Priest?* 29. Cupitt, *The Revelation of Being*, 99.

27 Cupitt, *The Revelation of Being*, 74.

28 Ibid., 94.

Ordinary Language

1 Cupitt, *The Revelation of Being*, 86.

2 Cupitt, *The New Religion of Life in Everyday Speech*, 111 n. 2.

3 Ibid., 50.

4 Griffiths, "Cupitt: Serious Thinker or Practical Joker?", 19.

5 Spearritt, review of *The New Religion of Life in Everyday Speech*, 7, quoting Cupitt, *The New Religion of Life in Everyday Speech*, 38.

6 Cupitt, *The Meaning of It All in Everyday Speech*, 41.

7 Cupitt, *Kingdom Come in Everyday Speech*, 113 n. 1.

8 Ibid., 64.

9 Ibid., 94.

The Religion of the Future

1 Cupitt, *Philosophy's Own Religion*, 168 n. 2. Cupitt is echoing here his earlier claim that theologians assert that "the end of dogmatism is the beginning of nihilism" (see "Anti-Realist Faith," in *Is God Real?* ed. Runzo, 49).

2 Hyman, *The Predicament of Postmodern Theology*, 22.

3 Milbank, Pickstock and Ward eds., *Radical Orthodoxy*, 1.

4 Cupitt, *After God*, 127.

5 Cupitt, *Philosophy's Own Religion*, viii–ix.

6 Ibid., 31.

7 Geering, *The World to Come*, 151.

8 Interestingly in the advertising for the Games of the XXVIIth Olympiad (Sydney 2000) sport was portrayed as embodying democratic, communal values as people of all races, creeds and genders "celebrate humanity." This agrees with Pierre de Coubertin's aim of the Olympics as "humanity's superior religion."

9 Cupitt, *Reforming Christianity*, 123.

10 Cupitt, *The Sea of Faith*, 111.

Conclusion

1 Myerson, "The Philosopher's Stone," 133.

2 Nineham, "In Praise of Solar Living," 5.

3 Cowdell, "The Recent Adventures of Don Cupitt," 35

4 Cupitt, *Philosophy's Own Religion*, xi.

5 Cupitt, "The Radical Christian World-View," 2.

Bibliography

Books

Allison, David B., ed. *The New Nietzsche*. Cambridge, Massachusetts: MIT Press, 1985.

Altizer, Thomas J. J., Max A. Myers, Carl A. Raschke, Robert P. Scharlemann, Mark C. Taylor, and Charles E. Winquist. *Deconstruction and Theology*. New York: Crossroad Publishing, 1982.

Anderson, Walter T., ed. *The Truth about the Truth: De-Confusing and Re-Constructing the Postmodern World*. New York: Penguin Putnam Books, 1995.

Armstrong, Karen. *A History of God*. London: Mandarin, 1994.

——— Don Cupitt, Arthur J. Dewey, Robert W. Funk, et al. *The Once and Future Faith*. Santa Rosa, California: Polebridge Press, 2001.

Basho, Matsuo. *The Narrow Road to the Deep North and Other Travel Sketches*. London: Penguin, 1966.

Bataille, Georges. *Blue of Noon*. Translated by Harry Mathews. London: Marion Boyars, 1986.

———. *Theory of Religion*. Translated by Robert Hurley. New York: Zone Books, 1989.

Beeson, Trevor. *Rebels and Reformers: Christian Renewal in the Twentieth Century*. London: SCM Press, 1999.

Berkeley, George. *Three Dialogues between Hylas and Philonous*. Edited by Colin M. Turbayne. New York: Bobbs Merrill Company, 1954.

Bowker, John. *Licensed Insanities: Religions and Belief in God in the Contemporary World*. London: Darton, Longman and Todd, 1987.

Braithwaite, R. B. *An Empiricist's View of the Nature of Religious Belief*. Cambridge: Cambridge University Press, 1955.

Brown, David. *Continental Philosophy and Modern Theology: An Engagement*. Oxford: Blackwell, 1987.

Bultmann, Rudolf. *Jesus Christ and Mythology*. New York: Charles Scribner's Sons, 1958.

Cabanne, Pierre. *Van Gogh*. London: Thames and Hudson, 1963.

Campbell, Lorne. *Rogier Van Der Weyden*. London: Harper and Row, 1980.

Caputo, John D. *The Mystical Element in Heidegger's Thought*. Athens, Ohio: Ohio University Press, 1978.

———. *Deconstruction in a Nutshell: A Conversation with Jacques Derrida*. New York: Fordham University Press, 1997.

———. *The Prayers and Tears of Jacques Derrida: Religion without Religion*. Bloomington and Indianapolis: Indiana University Press, 1997.

Carnley, Peter F. *The Structure of Resurrection Belief*. Oxford: Oxford University Press, 1987.

Clements, Keith W. *Lovers of Discord: Twentieth Century Theological Controversies in England*. London: SPCK, 1988.

Cottingham, John. *Descartes*. Oxford: Blackwell, 1986.

Cowdell, Scott. *Atheist Priest?: Don Cupitt and Christianity*. London: SCM Press, 1988.

———. *Is Jesus Unique?: A Study of Recent Christology*. New Jersey: Paulist Press, 1996.

———. *A God for this World*. London: Mowbray, 2000.

Crowder, Colin, ed. *God and Reality: Essays on Christian Non-Realism*. London: Mowbray, 1997.

Cupitt, Don. *Christ and the Hiddenness of God*. London: Lutterworth Press, 1971. 2nd ed. London: SCM Press, 1985.

———. *Crisis of Moral Authority*. London: Lutterworth Press, 1972.

———. *The Leap of Reason*. London: Sheldon Press, 1976. 2nd ed. London: SCM Press, 1985.

———. *Taking Leave of God*. London: SCM Press, 1980.

———. *The World to Come*. London: SCM Press, 1982. Xpress Reprints, London: SCM Press, 1993.

———. *The Sea of Faith*. London: BBC, 1984. 2nd ed. London: SCM Press, 1994.

———. *Only Human*. London: SCM Press, 1985.

———. *Life Lines*. London: SCM Press, 1986.

———. *The Long-Legged Fly: The Theology of Longing and Desire*. London: SCM Press, 1987. Xpress Reprints, London: SCM Press, 1995.

———. *The New Christian Ethics*. London: SCM Press, 1988. Xpress Reprints, London: SCM Press, 1996.

———. *Radicals and the Future of the Church*. London: SCM Press, 1989. Xpress Reprints, London: SCM, 1996.

———. *Creation out of Nothing*. London: SCM Press, 1990.

———. *What Is a Story?* London: SCM Press, 1991.

———. *The Time Being*. London: SCM Press, 1992.

———. *Rethinking Religion*. Wellington: St. Andrew's Trust for the Study of Religion and Society, 1992.

———. *After All: Religion without Alienation*. London: SCM Press, 1994.

———. *The Last Philosophy*. London: SCM Press, 1995.

———. *Solar Ethics*. London: SCM Press, 1995.

———. *After God: The Future of Religion*. London: Weidenfeld and Nicolson, 1997.

———. *Mysticism after Modernity*. Oxford: Blackwell, 1998.

_____. *The Religion of Being*. London: SCM Press, 1998.

_____. *The Revelation of Being*. London: SCM Press, 1998.

_____. *The New Religion of Life in Everyday Speech*. London: SCM Press, 1999.

_____. *The Meaning of It All in Everyday Speech*. London: SCM Press, 1999.

_____. *Kingdom Come in Everyday Speech*. London: SCM Press, 2000.

_____. *Philosophy's Own Religion*. London: SCM Press, 2000.

_____. *Reforming Christianity*. Santa Rosa, California: Polebridge Press, 2001.

_____. *Emptiness and Brightness*. Santa Rosa, California: Polebridge Press, 2001.

_____. *Is Nothing Sacred? The Non-Realist Philosophy of Religion: Selected Essays*. New York: Fordham University Press, 2002.

Dawes, Hugh. *Freeing the Faith: A Credible Christianity for Today*. London: SPCK, 1992.

Dawkins, Richard. *River Out of Eden: A Darwinian View of Life*. London: Phoenix, 1995.

Deleuze, Gilles. *Nietzsche and Philosophy*. Translated by Hugh Tomlinson. New York: Columbia University Press, 1983.

Derrida, Jacques. *Writing and Difference*. Translated by Alan Bass. Chicago: The University of Chicago Press, 1978.

Derrida, Jacques and Gianni Vattimo, eds. *Religion*. Cambridge: Polity Press, 1998.

Edwards, David L. *Tradition and Truth: The Challenge of England's Radical Theologians 1962–1989*. London: Hodder and Stoughton, 1989.

Farias, Victor. *Heidegger and Nazism*. Philadelphia: Temple University Press, 1989.

Feyerabend, Paul. *Against Method: An Outline of an Anarchistic Theory of Knowledge*. London: N.L.B., 1975.

Freeman, Anthony. *God in Us: A Case for Christian Humanism*. London: SCM Press, 1993.

Garvin, Harry R., ed. *Romanticism, Modernism, Postmodernism*. Lewisburg: Bucknell University Press, 1980.

Geering, Lloyd. *God in the New World*. London: Hodder and Stoughton, 1968.

_____. *Faith's New Age: A Perspective on Contemporary Religious Change*. London: Collins, 1980.

_____. *Creating The New Ethic*. Wellington: St. Andrew's Trust for the Study of Religion and Society, 1991.

_____. *Tomorrow's God: How We Create Our Worlds*. Wellington: Bridget Williams Books, 1994.

_____. *Does Society Need Religion?* Wellington: St. Andrew's Trust for the Study of Religion and Society, 1998.

_____. *The World to Come: From Christian Past to Global Future*. Santa Rosa, California: Polebridge Press, 1999.

_____. *Christianity without God*. Santa Rosa, California: Polebridge Press, 2002.

Gill, Carolyn B., ed. *Bataille: Writing the Sacred*. London: Routledge, 1994.

Gillespie, Michael Allen. *Nihilism before Nietzsche*. Chicago: The University of Chicago Press, 1995.

Goodchild, Philip. *Gilles Deleuze and the Question of Philosophy*. Madison: Farleigh Dickenson University Press, 1996.

Goulder, Michael, and John H. Hick. *Why Believe in God?* London: SCM Press, 1983.

Grenz, Stanley J. *A Primer on Postmodernism*. Grand Rapids, Michigan: Eerdmans, 1996.

Guignon, Charles, ed. *The Cambridge Companion to Heidegger*. Cambridge: Cambridge University Press, 1993.

Hamburger, Michael, trans. *The Poems of Paul Celan*. London: Anvil Press, 1988.

Hare, David. *Racing Demon*. Rev. ed. London: Faber and Faber, 1991.

Harries, Richard. *The Real God: A Response to Anthony Freeman's God in Us*. London: Mowbray, 1994.

Harris, Ian. *Creating God, Re-Creating Christ: Re-imagining the Christian Way in a Secular World*. Wellington: St. Andrew's Trust for the Study of Religion and Society, 1999.

Hart, David A. *Faith in Doubt: Non-Realism and Christian Belief*. London: Mowbray, 1993.

_____. *One Faith?: Non-Realism and the World of Faiths*. London: Mowbray, 1995.

_____. *Linking Up: Christianity and Sexuality*. Hertfordshire: Arthur James, 1997.

_____. ed. *Five Years of Making Waves*. Loughborough: Sea of Faith Network U.K., 1994.

Hart, Kevin. *The Trespass of the Sign: Deconstruction, Theology and Philosophy*. Cambridge: Cambridge University Press, 1989.

Hastings, Adrian. *A History of English Christianity: 1920–1990*. 3rd ed. London: SCM Press, 1991

_____. *The Shaping of Prophecy: Passion, Perception and Practicality*. London: Chapman, 1995.

Hayman, Ronald. *Nietzsche: A Critical Life*. London: Weidenfeld and Nicolson, 1980.

Hebblethwaite, Brian. *The Ocean of Truth: A Defence of Objective Theism*. Cambridge: Cambridge University Press, 1988.

_____. *Ethics and Religion in a Pluralistic Age: Collected Essays*. Edinburgh: T and T Clark, 1997.

Heidegger, Martin. *Basic Writings*. Edited by David F. Krell. London: Routledge and Kegan Paul, 1978.

_____. *An Introduction to Metaphysics*. Translated by Ralph Manheim. New Haven: Yale University Press, 1987.

_____. *Being and Time*. Translated by John Macquarrie and Edward Robinson. Oxford: Blackwell, 1967.

Hick, John. *Disputed Questions in Theology and the Philosophy of Religion*. New Haven, CT: Yale University Press, 1993.

_____, ed. *The Myth of God Incarnate*. London: SCM Press, 1977.

Holloway, Richard. *Dancing on the Edge*. London: Fount, 1997.

———. *Godless Morality: Keeping Religion Out of Ethics*. Edinburgh: Canongate, 1999.

———. *Doubts and Loves: What is Left of Christianity?* Edinburgh: Canongate, 2001.

House, Vaden D. *Without God or His Doubles: Realism, Relativism and Rorty*. New York: E. J. Brill, 1994.

Hume, David. *Dialogues and the Natural History*. Oxford: Oxford University Press (World's Classics), 1993.

Huntington, C. W. Jr. *The Emptiness of Emptiness*. Honolulu: University of Hawaii Press, 1989.

Hyman, Gavin. *The Predicament of Postmodern Theology: Radical Orthodoxy or Nihilist Textualism?* Louisville: Westminster John Knox Press, 2001.

James, Eric. *A Life of Bishop John A. T. Robinson: Scholar, Pastor, Prophet*. London: Collins, 1987.

Jencks, Charles. *What is Post-Modernism?* London: Academy Editions, 1989.

Jenkins, David, and Rebecca Jenkins. *Free to Believe*. London: BBC Books, 1991.

Kaufman, Gordon D. *God—Mystery—Diversity: Christian Theology in a Pluralistic World*. Minneapolis: Fortress Press, 1996.

Kaufmann, Walter. *Nietzsche: Philosopher, Psychologist, Antichrist*. 3rd ed. Princeton: Princeton University Press, 1968.

Kearney, Richard. *Dialogues with Contemporary Continental Thinkers: The Phenomenological Heritage*. Manchester: Manchester University Press, 1984.

Kerr, Fergus. *Theology after Wittgenstein*. Oxford: Blackwell, 1986.

Koelb, Clayton, ed. *Nietzsche as Postmodernist: Essays Pro and Contra*. New York: The State University of New York Press, 1990.

Krell, David F., ed. *Martin Heidegger — Basic Writings*. Rev. ed. San Francisco: HarperSanFrancisco, 1993

Lakeland, Paul. *Postmodernity: Christian Identity in a Fragmented Age*. Minneapolis: Fortress Press, 1997.

Land, Nick. *The Thirst for Annihilation: Georges Bataille and Virulent Nihilism*. London: Routledge, 1992.

Lawson, Hilary. *Closure: a story of everything*. London and New York: Routledge, 2001.

Lecercle, Jean-Jacques. *Philosophy through the Looking Glass*. La Salle, Illinois: Open Court, 1985.

Lindbeck, George A. *The Nature of Doctrine: Religion and Theology in a Postliberal Age*. Philadelphia: The Westminster Press, 1984.

Macquarrie, John. *Heidegger and Christianity*. New York: Continuum Publishing, 1994.

Madison, Gary B., ed. *Working Through Derrida*. Illinois: Northwestern University Press, 1993.

Magnus, Bernd and Kathleen M. Higgins, eds. *The Cambridge Companion to Nietzsche*. Cambridge: Cambridge University Press, 1996.

Malcolm, Norman. *Ludwig Wittgenstein: A Memoir*. Oxford: Oxford University Press, 1966.

――――. *Wittgenstein: A Religious Point of View?* Edited by Peter Winch. London: Routledge, 1993.

Mansel, Henry L. *The Limits of Religious Thought Examined*. 1859. Reprint, New York: AMS, 1973.

Mantle, Jonathan. *Archbishop: A Portrait of Robert Runcie*. London: HarperCollins, 1991.

MacDonald Smith, John. *On Doing without God*. Bicester: Emissary Publishing, 1993.

Megill, Allan. *Prophets of Extremity: Nietzsche, Heidegger, Foucault: Derrida*. Berkeley, California: University of California Press, 1985.

Miles, T. R. *Religion and the Scientific Outlook*. London: Macmillan Press, 1969.

――――. *Religious Experience*. London: Macmillan Press, 1972.

――――. *Speaking of God: Theism, Atheism and the Magnus Image*. York: Sessions of York, 1998.

Milbank, John. *Theology and Social Theory: Beyond Secular Reason*. Oxford: Blackwell, 1990.

Milbank, John, Catherine Pickstock, and Graham Ward, eds. *Radical Orthodoxy: A New Theology*. London: Routledge, 1999.

Monk, Ray. *Ludwig Wittgenstein: The Duty of Genius*. London: Vintage Books, 1991.

Moore, Gareth. *Believing in God: A Philosophical Essay*. Edinburgh: T and T Clark, 1988.

Murdoch, Iris. *Metaphysics as a Guide to Morals*. London: Chatto and Windus, 1992.

――――. *The Sovereignty of Good*. London: Routledge and Kegan Paul, 1970.

Murphy, John P. *Pragmatism: from Pierce to Davidson*. Boulder: Westview Press, 1990.

Nietzsche, Friedrich. *The Will to Power*. Translated by R J. Hollingdale and Walter Kaufmann. London: Weidenfeld and Nicolson, 1968.

――――. *Thus Spoke Zarathustra: A Book for Everyone and No One*. Translated by R. J. Hollingdale. 1961. Reprint with new introduction, London: Penguin, 1969.

――――. *Twilight of the Idols and the Anti-Christ*. Translated by R. J. Hollingdale. 1968. Reprint with a new introduction by Michael Tanner, London: Penguin, 1990.

――――. *Ecce Homo: How One Becomes What One Is*. Translated by R. J. Hollingdale. 1979. Reprint with a new introduction by Michael Tanner, London: Penguin, 1992.

Nineham, Dennis E. *Explorations in Theology 1*. London: SCM Press, 1977.

Nishitani Keiji. *Religion and Nothingness*. Translated by Jan Van Bragt. Berkeley and Los Angeles: University of California Press, 1982.

Ott, Hugo. *Martin Heidegger: A Political Life*. Translated by Allan Blunden. London: Fontana Press, 1994.

Pattison, George. *Art, Modernity and Faith: Restoring the Image*. 2nd ed. London: SCM Press, 1998.

———. *Kierkegaard and the Crisis of Faith*. London: SPCK, 1997.

———. *Agnosis: Theology in the Void*. London: Macmillan, 1996.

Patton, Paul, ed. *Deleuze: A Critical Reader*. Oxford: Blackwell, 1996.

Pears, David. *The False Prison: A Study of the Development of Wittgenstein's Philosophy*. Vol. 1. Oxford: Clarendon Press, 1987.

Perloff, Marjorie. *Wittgenstein's Ladder: Poetic Language and the Strangeness of the Ordinary*. Chicago: The University of Chicago Press, 1996.

Phillips, D. Z. *Religion without Explanation*. Oxford: Blackwell, 1976.

———. *Interventions in Ethics*. New York: State University of New York Press, 1992.

———. *Wittgenstein and Religion*. London: Macmillan Press, 1993.

———. *Faith after Foundationalism: Plantinga—Rorty—Lindbeck—Berger: Critiques and Alternatives*. Colorado: Westview Press, 1995.

Plato. *The Republic*. Rev. 2nd ed. Translated by Desmond Lee. London: Penguin, 1974.

Rapaport, Herman. *Heidegger and Derrida: Reflections on Time and Language*. Lincoln: University of Nebraska Press, 1989.

Richardson, Michael. *Georges Bataille*. London: Routledge, 1994.

Robinson, John A. T. *Where Three Ways Meet*. Edited by Eric James. London: SCM Press, 1987.

Rorty, Richard. *Contingency, Irony and Solidarity*. Cambridge: Cambridge University Press, 1989.

Rosen, Stanley. *The Question of Being: A Reversal of Heidegger*. New Haven: Yale University Press, 1993.

Runzo, Joseph, ed. *Is God Real?* New York: St. Martin's Press, 1993.

Sallis, John, ed. *Reading Heidegger: Commemorations*. Bloomington and Indianapolis: Indiana University Press, 1993.

Schacht, Richard. *Making Sense of Nietzsche: Reflections Timely and Untimely*. Urbana and Chicago: University of Illinois Press, 1995.

Scharlemann, Charles E. *Theology at the End of the Century*. Charlottesville: University Press of Virginia, 1990.

Schrift, Alan D. *Nietzsche and the Question of Interpretation: Between Hermeneutics and Deconstruction*. New York: Routledge, 1990.

———. *Nietzsche's French Legacy: Genealogy of Poststructuralism*. New York: Routledge, 1995.

Schutte, Ofelia. *Beyond Nihilism: Nietzsche without Masks*. Chicago: The University of Chicago Press, 1984.

Schweitzer, Albert. *My Life and Thought*. 2nd ed. Translated by C. T. Campion. London: Allen and Unwin, 1958.

Sedgwick, Peter R. *Nietzsche: A Critical Reader*. Oxford: Blackwell, 1995.

Shaw, Graham. *The Cost of Authority*. London: SCM Press, 1983.

———. *God in our Hands*. London: SCM Press, 1987.

Silverman, Hugh. J., ed. *Continental Philosophy 11: Derrida and Deconstruction*. London: Routledge, 1989.

Sluga, Hans, and David G. Stern, eds. *The Cambridge Companion to Wittgenstein*. Cambridge: Cambridge University Press, 1996.

Smith, Wilfred Cantwell. *The Meaning and End of Religion: A New Approach to the Religious Traditions of Mankind*. New York: Mentor, 1964.

Solomon, Robert C., and Kathleen M. Higgins, eds. *Reading Nietzsche*. New York: Oxford University Press, 1988.

Soskice, Janet Martin. *Metaphor and Religious Language*. Oxford: Clarendon Press, 1985.

Spong, John. S. *Why Christianity Must Change or Die: A Bishop Speaks to Believers in Exile*. San Francisco: HarperSanFrancisco, 1998.

Spong, John S. *Here I Stand: My Struggle for a Christianity of Integrity, Love and Equality*. San Francisco: HarperSanFrancisco, 2000.

Spong, John S. *A New Christianity For A New World*. San Francisco: HarperSanFrancisco, 2001.

Stambaugh, Jean. *Impermanence is Buddha Nature: Dogen's Understanding of Temporality*. Honolulu: University of Hawaii, 1990.

Sturrock, John, ed. *Structuralism and Since*. Oxford: Oxford University Press, 1979.

Tanner, Michael. *Nietzsche*. Oxford: OPUS, 1994.

Taylor, Mark C. *Altarity*. Chicago: The University of Chicago Press, 1987.

———. *About Religion: Economies of Faith in Virtual Culture*. Chicago: The University of Chicago Press, 1999.

Thiselton, Anthony C. *Interpreting God and the Postmodern Self: On Meaning, Manipulation and Promise*. Scottish Journal of Theology: Current Issues in Theology. Edinburgh: T and T Clark, 1995.

Thiel, John E. *Nonfoundationalism*. Minneapolis: Fortress Press, 1994.

Vardy, Peter. *The Puzzle of God*. London: Fount, 1995.

Ward, Graham. *Theology and Contemporary Critical Theory*. London: Macmillan Press, 1996.

———, ed. *The Postmodern God: A Theological Reader*. Oxford: Blackwell, 1997.

Ward, Keith. *Holding Fast to God: A Reply to Don Cupitt*. London: SPCK, 1982.

———. *The Turn of the Tide: Christian Belief in Britain Today*. London: BBC Publications, 1986.

Warnock, Mary. *Imagination and Time*. Oxford: Blackwell, 1994.

White, Stephen Ross. *Don Cupitt and the Future of Christian Doctrine*. London: SCM Press, 1994.

Williams, Stephen N. *Revelation and Reconciliation: A Window on Modernity*. Cambridge: Cambridge University Press, 1995.

Wilson, A. N. *God's Funeral*. London: Abacus, 2000.

Wittgenstein, Ludwig. *Tractatus Logico-Philosophicus*. Translated by D. F. Pears and
B. F. McGuiness. London: Routledge and Kegan Paul, 1961.
_____. *On Certainty*. Translated by Denis Paul and G. E. M. Anscombe. New
York: Harper and Row, 1969.
_____. *Philosophical Investigations*. Translated by G. E. M. Anscombe. Oxford:
Blackwell, 1974.
_____. *Culture and Value*. Translated by Peter Winch. Oxford: Blackwell, 1980.
Wolin, Richard, ed. *The Heidegger Controversy: A Critical Reader*. Cambridge,
Massachusetts: MIT Press, 1993.
Wright, Dale S. *Philosophical Meditations on Zen Buddhism*. Cambridge: Cambridge
University Press, 1998.
Wyer, Robert Van De. *Spinoza in a Nutshell*. London: Hodder and Stoughton,
1998.
Wyschogrod, Edith. *Saints and Postmodernism: Revisioning Moral Philosophy*.
Chicago: The University of Chicago Press, 1990.
_____. *An Ethics of Remembering: History, Heterology and the Nameless Others*.
Chicago: The University of Chicago Press, 1998.
Zeitlin, Irving M. *Nietzsche: A Re-Examination*. Cambridge: Polity Press, 1994.

Articles

Adams, Daniel. "Towards a Theological Understanding of Postmodernism."
Cross Currents 47, no. 4 (winter 1997). Online. Available: http://
www.aril.org/adams.html. 7 September 1999.
Altizer, Thomas. "Why So Conservative?" Paper presented at Sea of Faith U.K.
Conference X, University of Leicester, 1997. Online. Available:
http://www.sofn.org.uk/altiz97.html. 24 November 1999.
Brinkman, B. R. "'Outsidelessness' and 'High Noon.'" *The Heythrop Journal* 35, no.
1 (1994): 53–58.
Brummer, Vincent. "Has the Theism-Atheism Debate a Future?" *Theology* 97
(November/December 1994): 426–32.
Cairns, Adrian. "Inconclusions — for the Time Being." *Sea of Faith U.K. Magazine*,
no. 33 (summer 1998): 10–11.
Chapman, Mark. D. "Why the Enlightenment Project Doesn't Have to Fail." *The
Heythrop Journal* 39, no. 4 (1998): 379–93.
Cheetham, David. "Postmodern Freedom and Religion." *Theology* 103,
(January/February 2000): 29–36.
Clack, Beverley. "God and Language: A Feminist Perspective On the Meaning of
'God.'" In *The Nature of Religious Language: A Colloquium*, edited by Stanley E.
Porter, 148–158. Sheffield: Sheffield Academic Press, 1996.
Clark, Stephen R. L. Review of *Creation out of Nothing*, by Don Cupitt. *Religious
Studies* 27, no. 1 (1991): 559–61.
_____. "Cupitt and Divine Imagining." *Modern Theology* 5, no. 1 (1998): 45–60.

Cowdell, Scott. "The Recent Adventures of Don Cupitt." *St. Mark's Review*, no. 134 (winter 1988): 32–35.

_____. "Radical Theology, Postmodernity and Christian Life in the Void." *The Heythrop Journal* 32 (1991): 62–71.

_____. "All This, and God Too? Postmodern Alternatives to Don Cupitt." *The Heythrop Journal* 33 (1992): 267–82.

Crewdson, Joan. "Faith at Sea? A Critique of Don Cupitt's *After All: Religion Without Alienation*." *Modern Believing* 36, no. 3 (1995): 28–33.

Crowder, Colin. Review of *Atheist Priest?: Don Cupitt and Christianity*, by Scott Cowdell. *Modern Theology* 6, no. 3 (1990): 301–3.

Cupitt, Don. "Mansel's Theory of Regulative Truth." *Journal of Theological Studies* 18 (April 1967): 104–126.

_____ "How We Make Moral Decisions" *Theology* 76 (May 1973): 239–50.

_____. "God and Morality." *Theology* 76 (July 1973): 356–64.

_____. "On the Finality of Christ." In *The Leap of Reason*, 119–31. London: Sheldon Press 1976.

_____. "On Christian Existence in a Pluralist Society." In *The Leap of Reason*, 132–142. London: Sheldon Press, 1976.

_____. "Critical Christian Ethics." In *Explorations in Theology* 6, 87–97. London: SCM Press, 1979.

_____. "The Ethics of This World and the Ethics of the World to Come." In *Explorations in Theology* 6, 98–109. London: SCM Press, 1976.

_____. "Religion and Critical Thinking 2." *Theology* 86 (September, 1983): 328–35.

_____. "*The Sea of Faith*: the Backwash." *The Listener*, 1 November 1984, 24.

_____. "The Anglican Gorbachev." Review of *Robert* Runcie, by Adrian Hastings. *New Statesman and Society*, 25 January 1991, 35–36.

_____. "Dear God." *New Statesman and Society*, 20 December, 1991, 13–14.

_____. "After Liberalism." In *The Weight of Glory: A Vision and Practice for Christian Faith: The Future of Liberal Theology*, edited by D. W. Hardy and P. H. Sedgwick, 251–256. Edinburgh: T and T Clark, 1991.

_____. "Unsystematic Ethics and Politics." In *Shadow of Spirit: Postmodernism and Religion*, edited by Philippa Berry and Andrew Wernick, 149–55. London: Routledge, 1992.

_____. "Nature and Culture." In *Humanity, Environment and God*, edited by Neil Spurway, 33–45. Oxford: Blackwell, 1993.

_____. "Learning to Live with One Foot in the Grave." *The Guardian*, December 1993. Online. Available: http://www.sofn.org.uk/ofigrave.html. 4 September 1999.

_____. Review of *Kierkegaard and Modern Continental Philosophy: An Introduction*, by Michael Weston. *Religious Studies* 30, no. 4 (1994): 529–30.

_____. "All You Really Need Is Love." *The Guardian*, December 1994. Online. Available: http: www.sofn.org.uk/aynil.html. 4 September 1999.

_____. "Matters Eternal," *Financial Times*, 22/23 June 1996. Online. Available: http://www.sofn.org.uk/purity.html. 2 March 2000.

_____. "Friends, Faith and Humanism." *Sea of Faith (U.K.) Magazine*, no. 29 (summer 1997): 15–16.

_____. "My Postmodern Witch." *Modern Believing* 39, 4 (1998), 5–10.

_____. "Post-Christianity." In *Religion, Modernity and Postmodernity*, edited by Paul Heelas, 218–232. Oxford: Blackwell, 1998.

_____. "Magnus the Mastermind." *Sea of Faith (U.K.) Magazine*, no. 33 (summer 1998): 9.

_____. "A Democratic Philosophy of Life." Online. Available: http://www.sofn.org.uk.cuplist.html. 12 May 1999.

_____. "Religious and Non-Religious Humanism." Paper presented at the Sea of Faith U.K. Conference 1V, University of Leicester, 1991. Reprinted in *New Humanist* 106, no. 3 (September 1991): 11–12.

_____. "A Kingdom-Theology." Paper presented at the Sea of Faith Conference, New Zealand, 1994. Online. Available: http://www.geocities.com /Athens/Marble/1826/dckingdm.html. 29 March 2000.

_____. "Our Dual Agenda." Paper presented at the Sea of Faith U.K. Conference V11, University of Leicester, 1994. Online. Available: http://www.sofn.org.uk/dcdual.html. 12 February 2000.

_____. "World Religion." Paper presented at the Sea of Faith U.K. Conference 1X, University of Leicester, 1996.

_____. "From Religious Doctrine to Religious Experience." Paper presented at the Sea of Faith U.K. Conference X, University of Leicester, 1997.

_____. "Spirituality, Old and New." Paper presented at the Sea of Faith U.K. Conference X1, University of Sheffield, 1998.

_____. "The Radical Christian World-View." Paper presented at the Sea of Faith U.K. Conference X11, University of Leicester, 1999.

_____ "Saturday night fervour." *The Guardian* ("Face to Faith" series), April 3, 1999.

_____. "Christianity after the Church." Paper presented at the Sea of Faith U.K. Conference X111, University of Leicester, 2000.

_____ "Beyond Belief." Paper presented at the Sea of Faith in Australia Conference, Brisbane, October 2000.

_____ "Fear of ideas: The decline of Anglicanism." *The Guardian* ("Face to Faith" series), Saturday July 7, 2001.

_____. "Comparative Religions." *The Guardian* ("Face to Faith" series), Saturday 27th October, 2001.

_____. "The Simpsons in search of Jesus." *The Guardian* ("Face to Faith" series), February 24, 2001.

_____. "An Apologia for my thinking." Paper presented at the multi-faith centre at the University of Derby, 11th May 2002.

Dyson, Anthony. Review of *The New Christian Ethics*, by Don Cupitt. *Theology* 92 (September 1989): 538–39.

Evans, Stephen C. "Realism and Anti-Realism in Kierkegaard's Concluding Unscientific Postscript." In *The Cambridge Companion to Kierkegaard*, edited by Alistair Hannay and Gordon D. Marino, 154–76. Cambridge: Cambridge University Press, 1998.

Gaskin, J. C. A. "Absolute Relativism." *The Expository Times* 104 (October 1992—September 1993): 191.

Griffiths, Leslie. "Cupitt: Serious Thinker or Practical Joker?" *Sea of Faith (U.K.) Magazine*, no. 38 (autumn 1999): 19.

Hampson, Daphne. Review of *The Religion of Being*, by Don Cupitt. *Theology* 102 (March/April, 1999): 131–32.

Hart, David A. "On Not Quite Taking Leave of Don." *Modern Believing* 35, no. 4 (1994): 6–9.

———. Review of *Solar Ethics*, by Don Cupitt. Online. Available: http://www.sofn.org.uk/solar.html. 20 August 1999.

Hart, Kevin. "Nietzsche, Derrida and Deconstructing the True Gospel." *Zadok Perspectives*, no. 60 (autumn 1998): 8–11.

Hey, John. Review of *Solar Ethics*, by Don Cupitt. *Theology* 99 (September/October 1996): 394.

Hollywood, Amy. "'Beautiful as a Wasp': Angela of Foligno and Georges Bataille." *Harvard Theological Review* 92 no. 2 (April 1999): 219–36.

Hyman, Gavin. "Towards a New Religious Dialogue: Buddhism and Postmodern Theology." *The Heythrop Journal* 39, no. 4 (October 1998): 394–413.

———. 'D. Z. Phillips: The Elusive Philosopher.' *Theology*, 102 (July/August 1999): 271–78.

James, Eric. Review of *Taking Leave of God*, by Don Cupitt. *The Times*, 10 February 1981, 10.

Jenkins, David. Review of *Radicals and the Future of the Church*, by Don Cupitt. *Theology* 94 (January/February 1991): 60–61.

Jones, Richard. Review of *The New Christian Ethics*, by Don Cupitt. *The Expository Times* 100 (October 1988–September 1989): 306–7.

Leaves, Nigel. "Be(com)ing an atheist country? Pastoral and theological implications from an Australian perspective *after* Don Cupitt." *Colloquium: The Australian and New Zealand Theological Review*, Volume 31 No. 1 (May 1999), 21–30.

Mark, James. Review of *Taking Leave of God*, by Don Cupitt. *Theology* 84 (May 1981): 211–13.

Mullen, Peter. "Serial Theology." *Theology* 86 (January 1983): 25–29.

Myerson, George. "The Philosopher's Stone: A Response to Don Cupitt." *History of the Human Sciences* 11, no. 3 (1998): 131–36.

Nineham, Dennis. "In Praise of Solar Living." Review of *After God*, by Don Cupitt. *Times Literary Supplement*, 26 December 1997, 5.

Nolan, Steve. Review of *The Religion of Being*, by Don Cupitt. *Reviews on Religion and Theology* 4, no. 4 (1998): 51–54.

Olds, Mason. "Don Cupitt's Ethics." *Religious Humanism* 28, no.2 (spring 1994): 73–85.

Paterson, Torquil. "Why I Resigned." Unpublished Paper.

Pattison, George. "Editorial: *The Sea of Faith* — Ten Years After." *Modern Believing* 35, no. 4 (1994): 2–5.

Pearse, Ronald. "How Myth Could Enrich the Spirit," *The Times* (London), 23 February 1985.

Phillips, D. Z. "Theological Castles and the Elusiveness of Philosophy — A Reply." *Theology* 102 (November/December1999): 436–41.

Pickstone, Charles. "We Are Grateful to Don Cupitt: Don Cupitt on Art." *Modern Believing* 35, no. 4 (1994): 10–17.

Runzo, Joseph. "Ethics and the Challenge of Theological Non-Realism." In *Ethics, Religion, and the Good Society*, edited by Joseph Runzo, 72–91. Kentucky: Westminster/John Knox Press, 1992.

Russell, Brian. "With Respect to Don Cupitt." *Theology* 88 (January 1985): 5-11.

Schacht, Richard. "After Transcendence: The Death of God and the Future of Religion." In *Religion without Transcendence?* edited by D. Phillips and Timothy Tessin, 73–92. London: Macmillan Press, 1997.

Shakespeare, Steven. "The New Romantics: A Critique of Radical Orthodoxy." *Theology* 103 (May/June 2000): 163–77.

Sheehan, Thomas. "Heidegger and the Nazis." *The New York Review of Books*, 16 June 1988, 38–47.

———. "A Normal Nazi." *The New York Review of Books*, 14 January 1993, 30–35.

Spearritt, Gregory. "Christianity: From Modernism to Postmodernism." *Colloquium* 24, no. 2 (1992): 67–81.

———. "Don Cupitt: Christian Buddhist?" *Journal of Religious Studies* 31 (1995): 359–73.

———. Review of *The New Religion of Life in Everyday Speech*, by Don Cupitt. *Sea of Faith in Australia Bulletin*, May 1999, 7.

Sutherland, Stewart. "En route for the Ineffable." *The Times Literary Supplement*, 28th May, 1982, 574.

Tarbox J. Jr., Everett. "The A/Theology of Don Cupitt: A Theological Option in Our Post-Modern Age." *Religious Humanism* 35, no. 2 (spring 1991): 72–82.

———. "Beyond Postmodern: Don Cupitt's Theology of Expressionism." *Religious Humanism* 28, no. 2 (spring 1994): 55–72.

Turner, Denys. "De-Centring Theology." *Modern Theology* 2, no. 2 (1986): 125–43.

Ward, Graham. Review of *The Last Philosophy*, by Don Cupitt. *Theology* 98 (November/December 1995): 477–78.

———. "Theology and Postmodernism." *Theology* 100 (November/December 1997): 435–40.

Wiles, Maurice. Review of *Mysticism after Modernity*, by Don Cupitt. *Theology* 101 (September/October 1998): 392–93.

Wilson, Kenneth. Review of *The Revelation of Being*, by Don Cupitt. *Reviews in Religion and Theology* 3, no. 3 (1999): 328–30.

Williams, Rowan. "Religious Realism: On Not Quite Agreeing with Don Cupitt." *Modern Theology* 1, no. 1 (1984): 3–24.

Wyschogrod, Edith, and Caputo, John D. "Postmodernism and the Desire for God: An E-Mail Exchange." *Cross Currents* 48, no. 3 (fall 1998). Online. Available: http://www.crosscurrents.org/caputo.html. 7 September 1999.

Yam, Philip. "Exploiting Zero-Point Energy." *Scientific American* 277, no. 6 (1997): 82–85.

York, Anne. "Wittgenstein's Later Mysticism." *Theology* 100 (September/October 1997): 352–63.

Dissertation and Radio Talks/Interviews

Cupitt, Don. "Faith in Future." Lent Talk, BBC Radio 4, April 2000.

Cupitt, Don. Interview by Rachael Kohn. *Post-Millennial Prophets: The Spirit of Things*. ABC Radio, 16 May 1999.

Vitalis, Hugo. "The Sea of Faith Network (NZ): A Non-Realist Alternative to Christian Realism." Master's Thesis: Victoria University, Wellington, New Zealand, 1994.

Index